GW00503641

JOWETTS
OF THE 1920s

NOEL STOKOE

AMBERLEY

First published 2013

Amberley Publishing
The Hill, Stroud
Gloucestershire, GL5 4EP

www.amberley-books.com

Copyright © Noel Stokoe, 2013

The right of Noel Stokoe to be identified as the Author
of this work has been asserted in accordance with the
Copyrights, Designs and Patents Act 1988.

All rights reserved. No part of this book may be reprinted
or reproduced or utilised in any form or by any electronic,
mechanical or other means, now known or hereafter invented,
including photocopying and recording, or in any information
storage or retrieval system, without the permission in writing
from the Publishers.

British Library Cataloguing in Publication Data.
A catalogue record for this book is available from the British Library.

ISBN 978 1 4456 1429 8
E-BOOK ISBN 978 1 4456 1433 5

Typesetting and Origination by Amberley Publishing.
Printed in Great Britain.

Introduction

William and Benjamin Jowett were the sons of Wilfred Jowett, a blacksmith living and working at 87 Kensington Street, Girlington, Bradford. He had five children, Ruth Elizabeth (1875), Benjamin (1877), Joseph (1878), William (1880), and Beatrice Anne (1882). Wilfred's wife, Sarah, died in 1888, and Joseph died in infancy prior to her. Benjamin and William found themselves helping their father in the blacksmith's business, and were involved in repairs of anything mechanical. By the late 1890s they were working for him full time.

Benjamin and William had a dream of building their own car and became more and more involved in engine repairs. In 1901, Benjamin, William and Ruth left the family home to set up their own business 'The Jowett Motor Manufacturing Company', based in Church Street, Bradford, each investing £30. The brothers for some time had wanted to produce a better engine with less noise and vibration for existing cars, in particular the De Dion and Aster. During this period, Arthur Lamb joined the business by buying Ruth's third share at £60, as the concern was valued at £180. He was a well-known cycle engineer, but was to undertake clerical duties, which allowed the brothers to concentrate on engine design. The business moved in 1904 to larger premises nearby at Back Burlington Street, off Manningham Lane, Bradford, as access was difficult and space was at a premium in the old premises.

Experiments continued with engine design, and in 1905 they produced a twin-cylinder horizontally-opposed unit, which was rated at 6.4 horsepower. This engine was used in the first prototype tiller-steered car built by the brothers and registered AK 494 on 14 February 1906. The car was used and tested by the brothers extensively over the next four years. Other engines were also tested but the engine in the prototype proved to be the best. A local coachbuilder called Ryder built the body for the car, described by the Jowett brothers as the world's first purpose-built 'light car', a justifiable claim, as it only weighed 6cwt. The general engineering side of the business continued to grow rapidly, and by 1907 the Church Street premises had been outgrown. Fortunately, the brothers were offered the premises of Grosvenor Road, Bradford, giving them the much-needed space to expand their business.

By early 1910, the brothers felt the car had been tested enough, and that it should be put into production. The first batch of twelve cars was built between 1910 and 1911 they still retained the tiller steering, but now had a small flat boot, unlike the prototype body which ended at the rear of the seat.

The brothers soon realised that with the low RAC rating of 6.4hp, it was causing public resistance, as people at the time felt a car was inferior if it was too small. In true Yorkshire fashion the brothers altered the advertising to read a rating of 8hp, even though no alteration was made to the car at all. This did the trick as sales then took off and never looked back!

Between 1912 and 1916 a further thirty-six cars were built, with many modifications and improvements being made, the most noticeable of which was the introduction of a steering wheel in 1914 in place of the tiller steering. This was probably the last production car to switch from tiller to a steering wheel.

By the end of 1916 all car production ceased, and the factory was used during the war for producing armaments and manufacturing machinery. Small components were also produced for the Rolls-Royce 'Eagle' Aero Engine and brake shoes for Crossley and Albion Motors. This was a profitable time for the brothers, but was also a great help to the war effort.

After the war Benjamin wanted to form a new company, and build a new purpose-built factory for the reinstatement of car production. A worked-out stone quarry was found on the northern outskirts of Bradford at Five Lane Ends, Idle. It was looked at and purchased by the brothers. This site, at the time, was in open country, but was on the tram link into Bradford.

Things moved quickly and the new factory was built during 1919 and measured 100 feet by 150 feet. The new company, 'Jowett Cars Ltd', was registered on 30 June 1919, and light engineering work was still carried out at the Grosvenor Road property by the Jowett Motor Manufacturing Company Ltd, and would become the main sales outlet for Jowett Cars Ltd. At the end of 1919, lathes, milling machines and other equipment were transferred from the Grosvenor Road works to the new premises in Idle. Also many items of Government surplus machinery were purchased including brazing hearths, blacksmiths forge, and a case-hardening plant, enabling car production to commence in April 1920.

By the end of the year, approximately 100 Two-Seater cars were built, these were effectively a Short-Two without a dickey seat, but they were not described as that until 1923. It was still the same model that was produced in 1921, but with an increased production figure of 249. There were two models offered in 1922, the Two-Seater and the Two-Seater Deluxe; the Deluxe was fitted with the dickey seat. Once again the production figure increased to 492 this year. 1923 saw the Short-Two model, which was the Two-Seater Deluxe model, the original Two-Seater was now dropped. There was also the introduction of the Long-Four and the 4cwt Short-Chassis Van, total production increased again to 1,047. 1924 saw four models in production, the Short-Two with dickey, Long-Four, 4cwt Short-Chassis Van and the 5cwt Long-Chassis Van; total production figures for the year also increased to 1,853. 1925 saw the Short-Two, Long-Four, Short-Four (Chummy), 4cwt Short-Chassis Van and the 5cwt Long-Chassis Van; total production figures for the year increased again to 2,223.

Moving to the second half of the decade, 1926 saw the model range increase again, Short-Two with dickey, Short-Four (Chummy), Long-Four, Saloon, Short Chassis Two-

Seater with box at rear, 4cwt Short Chassis van, 5cwt Long Chassis van, 2cwt Long Chassis Two-Seater with box at rear; the total production for the year being 2,064. The number of models available in 1927 increased again, Short-Two with dickey, Long-Two with dickey, Short-Four (Chummy), Long-Four, Saloon, 4cwt Short Van , 5cwt Long Van, Short Chassis Two-Seater with box at rear, Long Chassis Two-Seater with box at rear, there was also a massive increase in production this year to 3,474. There were even more models to chose from in 1928, Short-Two with dickey, Long-Two with dickey, Long Coupé with dickey, Sports model, Short-Four (Chummy), Long-Four, Coachbuilt Saloon, Fabric Saloon, 4cwt Short Van, 5cwt Long Van, Long Chassis Two-Seater, with box, 5cwt Long-Four Tourer adapted for goods transportation with opening tailgate, 5cwt Lorry, Sundry Special Army Vehicles (sixteen built); the total production this year fell back to 2,029. There was also a substantial model range for 1929 which included the Short-Four Chummy, Short Saloon, Long-Two with dickey, Long-Four Fabric Body, Long-Four Coachbuilt, Long-Four Saloon Fabric, Long-Four Saloon Coachbuilt, Black Prince Deluxe, 6cwt Long Lorry, 6cwt Long Van, 5cwt Dual-Purpose Traveller's Car, Long Coupé with dickey, Long Chassis Two-Seater with box, total production for this year being 2,652. The total production figure for the decade amounted to 16,183, this figure included Short and Long Chassis only, which were also available each year from 1922 and 1925 respectively.

It is noticeable how many extra models appeared from 1927, but many of these were in very small numbers such as the Long Coupé with dickey where only seventy were built between 1928 and 1929, Sports model in 1928 where fourteen were produced, also in 1928, sixteen various army vehicles, twenty-nine Dual Purpose Travellers cars in 1929 and the Long Chassis Two-Seater with Box, where only six were built between 1928 and 1929.

Sadly there are no survivors of several of these models, such as the Long Coupé with dickey, the Dual Purpose Travellers car and the Sports model. Over the last thirty years or so, however, there has been a huge revival in interest in the Vintage Jowett and many restorations have taken place, several of which will be featuring in this book.

A 1920 Jowett Two-Seater, which along with the 1921 model, was the only model available offered by the Jowett brothers after car production recommenced in April 1920. This model did not have the opening dickey seat as this was not offered until the Two-Seater Deluxe was introduced in 1922 and was a great success, so the original model was dropped and the Two-Seater Deluxe then became known as the Short-Two. Only 100 1920 models were produced between April 1920 and December 1920, with a further 249 in 1921.

This picture of a 1922 Short-Two was taken by me at the Jowett Car Club National Rally in York in 1974 and in many ways was a turning point in my life. Jane and I had lived in York up to our marriage in 1972, we then moved to Riccall, near Selby about fifteen miles away. I had heard that there was an old car rally on York Racecourse, so I took my Dad, who was an old car enthusiast. This event turned out to be a JJC event and had Jowetts of every shape and size including this 1922 model right through to the R1 Jupiter of 1952. This convinced me that I wanted to own an old car, and as I was a Yorkshireman, a Jowett seemed the obvious choice. It was out of the question at that time as we had just had our first child, Jonathan, so I had more pressing responsibilities, then Jessica and Ben followed. I got the old-car-bug again in 1984, thinking it was now or never! I joined the Jowett Club in August 1984 and bought my first Jowett – a Jupiter in February 1985, which I still have. Since then I have added a Javelin saloon and a Bradford Utility, which have brought me great pleasure over the years. My Dad is seen here talking to the owner, a young Dennis Mitchell, who is still a club member. Sadly my Dad died a few months after this picture was taken, so never saw me buy a Jowett; ironically this Short-Two now lives near Whitby about seven miles away from me!

These pictures are of the same car taken at a rally recently; it shows the attractive lines of the car which makes it a model that is greatly sought after today. In fact, the demand for the car is so great that cars are being restored now which would only have been regarded as parts-cars a few years ago.

Top and middle: By mid-1922 the Jowett brothers realised there would be a strong market for small commercial vehicles for small businesses such as shopkeepers and sales reps, etc. The first commercial produced that year was the 4cwt short-chassis model; this was followed by the 5cwt long-chassis model. This is a 1923 5cwt Long-Chassis model which was the object of a heroic restoration a few years ago. This model was produced right through the 1920s, but as far as I am aware of, this is the only survivor. It was seen here at the Jowett Car Club Ex-Employees meeting at the Bradford Industrial Museum in August 2008.

Bottom: During the early 1920s a new spectator sport appeared in the shape of car reliability runs and freak hill climbs and spectators would come out in vast numbers to watch these events. Ben and William Jowett both took part in trials as early as 1921. The Jowett proved ideally suited for this arduous pastime as it was strong and rugged and had fantastic hill-climbing qualities. Another early trials driver was Major J. D. Johnstone, who commissioned this special light-weight sports model from the Jowett brothers. This car was used extensively during the 1920s in events such as the MCC 'Land's End' Trial and the 1924 RSAC 'Light Car Trials'. (LAT Photographic)

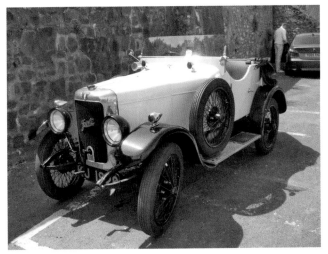

This is the same car today, owned by William Jowett's Grandson, Mike Koch-Osborne. The car had been laid-up for many years, but Mike knew of its location and was eventually able to purchase it. The car is original in every way and looks great!

This 1923 Short-Two appeared at the club's National Rally at Llandrindod Wells in 2012, this was of great interest to many club members, including myself, as it was the first time a lot of us had seen it.

Look what happens when a 'new' Jowett is spotted! This is another view of the above 1923 Short-Two. (Tony Fearn)

This is a lovely period picture of a *c.* 1924 Short-Two taken in St Peter's Street in Hereford in 1925, this is a Francis Firth Collection picture and I am most grateful to them for allowing me to use this image in this book.

A 1923 Short-Two taking part in a reliability trial. (Jowett Car Club Archive)

The Jowett brothers were always on the look-out for good ways of obtaining publicity for their cars, if this could be done free or with minimal expense, so much the better! A good example of this came about in 1924, when a new sewerage system was to be opened between Bradford and Esholt. The mayoral party wanted to lay the last brick, which required a journey of three miles down a narrow sewerage tunnel in cars. Needless to say the Jowett brothers jumped at the challenge and laid on four long-fours for the ceremony, which made the trip without incident. This picture shows one of the cars after it had made emerged after making this three mile trip. (Jowett Car Club Archive)

Another of the mayoral party pictured within one of the tunnels. (Jowett Car Club Archive)

'Jowett's Subterranean Tour – How Four Light Cars were driven Three Miles along an Underground Tunnel', *The Light Car & Cyclecar*, 17 October 1924

Imagine a brick tunnel, ten feet in diameter, buried in parts nearly 400 feet below the ground, illuminated only by the very local glare of car headlamps and filled with weird noises from the intermingled exhausts of four light cars, and some idea will be gained of a unique underground journey recently accomplished by a small fleet of Jowetts.

The tunnel in question is part of a £3,000,000 sewage scheme originally embarked upon by the City of Bradford about 11 years ago. It was three miles long, and connects Bradford with Esholt, while it cost £500,000 to build.

Recently, when the tunnel was completed, it was proposed to take a number of officials through it and perform an opening ceremony in the centre by placing the last brick in position. The problem arose: How were the officials to reach the centre of the tunnel? Walking was out of the question, because the interior was naturally slimy and a miniature watercourse ran along the bottom. It was thought that cars might be used for the purpose, but experiments with a well-known make suggested that their use would be out of the question, and it was decided to take officials and visitors through the tunnel in pony carriages.

Jowett Offer Accepted

Jowett Cars Ltd hearing of this suggestion, promptly undertook to carry out the necessary transport arrangements – naturally, with cars of their own manufacture. This offer was accepted. In rehearsing the proceedings it was found, after patient practice, that a speed of over 20mph in top gear could be maintained along the tunnel, despite the fact that the sides on which the wheels rested were at a gradient of 1 in 2.3. This gradient, combined with the extremely slippery surface, made driving very difficult, and an error of judgement might have led at any moment to one of the cars capsizing – an awkward predicament in the circumstances.

One of the drivers, describing his experiences to us, said that the smallest deviation from a direct course had to be instantly corrected, as any inaccuracy or change of direction was violently progressive in seriousness, the car feeling as though it wanted to loop the loop sideways.

The negotiating of the tunnel is, of course, only one of a considerable number of unusual stunts which have been carried out from time to time in Jowett cars in the past, but it must be admitted that none previously has been of quite so original a nature.

A Creditable Performance

Although not a test likely to be required of light cars in general, the tunnel performance is, nevertheless, of interest, in that it clearly indicates the controllability and the capacity of the modern light car to go anywhere, while it naturally reflects considerable credit on the Jowett cars which took part, especially in view of the fact that before the Jowett Company took up the matter the event had every appearance of being abandoned.

This, perhaps, is the first occasion on which cars have been used for long journeys underground, and we certainly never heard before of small cars being driven at a depth of 400 feet below the surface of the earth.

The designing of the new works of which the tunnel is a part, was the task of Mr Joseph Garfield M Inst CE, the sewage works engineer, and his assistant, Mr Howard Wonter-Smith M Inst CE, the work having been carried out under the chairmanship of Alderman R. Johnson, who performed the opening ceremony.

'Three Miles Through a Sewer – Four small cars convey Bradford Municipal Officials on a Tour of Inspection', *The Autocar*, 24 October 1924

At the recent opening of a new sewage works for the Bradford Corporation a problem arose as the transport of the civic officials and many civil engineer visitors through a three-mile tunnel from Bradford to Esholt and back for the opening and inspection ceremony.

The sewer is ten-foot in diameter, and although it had not been put in service, it was wet and slippery. The first attempt to use motor cars for the purpose of conveying the members of the inspection party failed; pony carts were then suggested, but the situation was saved by Jowett Motors Ltd., of Idle, Bradford, who undertook to do the work. Four four-seater Jowett cars were commissioned, and in these the various officials and visitors concerned were transported through the tube in batches of sixteen.

The drivers experienced little difficulty except at speeds over 8mph, when the cars evidenced a rather pronounced tendency to climb up the sloping sides of the tunnel.

Built of brick the tunnel is a circular tube, three miles long with a seven foot drop in the total distance. The use of the Jowett cars for the inspection trip was quite successful.

Top and middle: The next two pictures show a 1924 Short-Two, the one from the rear with the hood down shows the opening dickey seat. The grey paint and black wings work well.

Bottom: Mr C. L. Wade contacted the club website in June 2002 saying, 'The following may be of interest to you; I have come across this photograph of my uncle at the side of a Jowett Car. The registration number is W-149, which is Sheffield I think. I do not know if he actually owned it. His name was Hubert Coldwell, and he lived at 153 St Lawrence Rd, Tinsley, Sheffield. The house is still there, but the photograph was not taken there. Date I would think around 1925, note the Union Jack.'

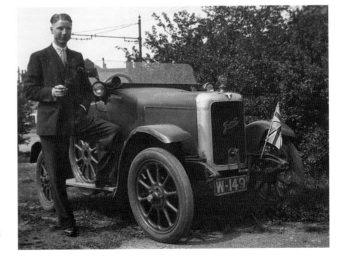

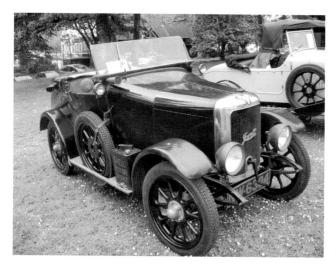

Another 1924 Short-Two,
this time in maroon with
black wings.

The next four pictures show how a 1925 Short-Two was restored in New Zealand in 2012 by Vic Morrison. The first picture shows the dismantled, but basically complete car piled up onto Vic's trailer.

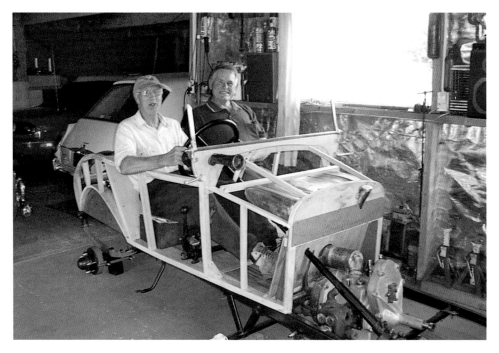

The car is now starting to take shape again with the chassis and mechanicals restored with the basic body framework in place.

The aluminum bodywork has now been fabricated and ready to be assembled onto the car.

The finished car back on the road and looking good.

Rebirth of a 1925, Vic Morrison, New Zealand, January 2013

The phone rang and a voice said, 'Would you be interested in the bits of my 1925 Jowett!' Long pause! I knew the car and thought of the expense and the work needed to restore the mechanicals and to build a body for it. I answered, 'No, but I would see if I could find a suitable home for it.'

Over a coffee my wife, Maureen, said 'Why don't you buy it, you would enjoy doing it and it will keep you out of trouble!' I drew up a list of questions to ask in order to refresh my memory and rang back. 'Does it have a chassis?' 'No!' This was not a good start I thought. But it has the front bit and the back bit. Story goes that someone wanted to build a lathe and cut the straight bits out for the bed! Most other bits were there including the hood mechanism and even the seats or what was left of them. I made an offer and the bits were mine!

This car was taken off the road after the Second World War because the owner couldn't get tyres for it. It was taken apart and stored under a house in Auckland. The only body pieces kept were the dickey seat door and the passenger door on the left side of the car, the only door on this model. However, the aluminium that covered the scuttle or bulkhead was rolled up amongst the stuff. It all stayed there until the owner died and in 1982 Bruce MacFarlane, an owner of a Jowett Javelin was approached by the son to see if he wanted this old Jowett. He collected everything that was there and stored it in a dry garage until I got it in May 2010. The Auckland Jowett boys crated it all up on a double pallet and shipped it to a freight depot in Christchurch from where I picked it up on a large trailer bringing it back to where we live in Whitecliffs, which is an hour away. It was very exciting unpacking it all to see what I had actually bought. I was generally more than satisfied although there was certainly some work to do.

I started work first on the rear axle assembly. Because the foot brake works on the driveshaft, this is very hard on the crownwheel and pinion so it was no surprise to find a tooth missing on the pinion. This was cleverly repaired by Duralloy in Christchurch. Carrier and wheel bearings were good but I replaced all pinion bearings. The front axle was next, needing new kingpins which I made and just one wheel bearing. Despite it coming with several wheels only one could be used. A search of the Vintage Car Club's parts in Christchurch revealed two usable wheels thankfully and I modified one I had to suit, getting another from a fellow Jowetteer. The four springs were taken apart leaf by leaf, cleaned up and reassembled making new shackle pins and bushes along with the brass grease nipples. The missing centre section of the chassis was made to match the ends, which were then professionally welded in place, looking quite correct and strong when finished. Soon we had wheels beneath it, always a milestone in any restoration.

Now to the engine, which I completely dismantled and was amazed to find it in very good condition, still standard and hardly any wear apart from the valve guides which were the only things I had to replace. The pistons were cast iron of course with wide rings which were so good I used them again. All this reminded me of Jowett's advertising slogan, 'Jowetts never wear out, they are left to next of kin!' The gearbox similarly was in great condition not even needing bearings, just a wash and back together again. It has a very clever and neat gearchange and handbrake assembly, which is operated on the right hand side of the car, there being no driver's door of course. Jowett Parts in England supplied the two fabric universals for the driveshaft. We now came to the radiator and this was a real challenge. It does not have a core as such, just thirty-six tubes in two rows with hundreds of square fins on the front and eighteen tubes and the same number of round ones on the rear tubes. Nothing could be salvaged. Luckily I found a clever engineer who also makes old radiators and he was going to make the dies needed to stamp out the fins and solder to new tubes but with a stroke of luck I was able to get thirty-six tubes complete with fins from a similarly clever chap in England. My man fitted these to the radiator shell after he made one from two (fellow Jowetteer to the rescue again). The shell is German Silver and buffed up like new. All we needed now was a body.

Being a Jowett enthusiast of some fifty years I have collected a lot of data on the various models and among these was a factory drawing of the framework for the body of my car which gave me a lot of information but alas no measurements. However, the bonnet gave me the start and shape of the scuttle, the original aluminium piece gave me the length, the windscreen frame determined the width, the backrest of the seat gave me the width at this point and the dickey seat door gave the size and shape for the back of the car. Likewise the passenger's door gave the curve of the body and the shaping of the side of the car. For the right side I used a mirror image. I am confident I have a pretty exact copy. There was quite a lot of work in all this and it all had to be faired from all ways so the aluminium would cover it nicely. Finally that day came and a good mate of mine gave me a hand to panel it, taking a full day. Just as we finished a vice-grip that we were using to hold a straightedge, flew off and landed in the scuttle of the body which was upside down at the time. It made a small dent in our otherwise pristine body. Bugger and damn! Once we had the body the right way up I thought just a wee tap with hammer and dolly would sought it but the more I tapped the worse it got until there was quite a bulge. I had to sit my hat over the bulge to hide it so I wouldn't get too depressed when I came into the garage! The four guards needed lots of new metal and a significant amount of work to bring them up standard. This work was done by a local man with me acting as sander. One bonnet side was missing so he made another along with new running board valances using the battered originals as patterns. He also managed to get rid of the bulge too and then he painted the body a nice fawn colour which was the colour of the car when it was dismantled all those years ago. The guards and valances were painted black and once assembled it looked very smart. I had a new seat made to the original pattern but was able to salvage the original dickey seat. There was just enough of the hood material for a pattern so I had a new hood sewn up and after sorting the hinging mechanism and making new bows I fitted the new hood material using the original rear window frame albeit with new perspex.

Time now for it to become road legal so after some fettling I was happy to drive it the fifty miles to Christchurch for the process which it passed with flying colours. Luckily there was the old six-figure steel front number plate amongst the bits and although their records didn't go this far back they accepted that it had been previously registered in New Zealand. So now that I was able to motor legally, I gradually sorted little things so that it now is a lovely wee car to drive and the right hand gear change is a delight up and down the box when you get those revs just right.

Altogether a most satisfying result from a pile of rusty bits!

I spotted this nice period shot showing the proud owner of a c. 1925 Long-Four with his family on the Sussex Vintage Vehicle Society website. The picture was sent to them for identification by Trevor Harvey, it was taken at Ottershaw, and he thinks the lady on the left looks like his grandmother Harvey. The registration number TW 715 was issued by Essex CC from 1925 – clearly, women were not frightened to wear fur in those days! (SVVS)

As mentioned before, Jowetts also built light commercials alongside its range of cars. This is a 1925 4cwt Short-Chassis van and has been the subject of a complete restoration over many years which is now nearing completion. Once again, this is the only survivor of this particular model.

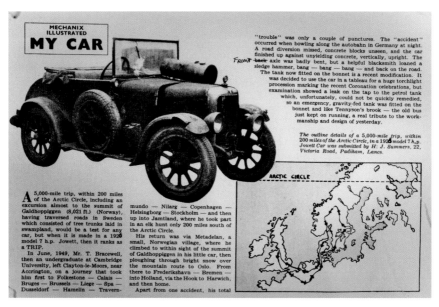

MECHANIX ILLUSTRATED
MY CAR

"trouble" was only a couple of punctures. The "accident" occurred when bowling along the autobahn in Germany at night. A road diversion missed, concrete blocks unseen, and the car finished up against unyielding concrete, vertically, upright. The FRONT back axle was badly bent, but a helpful blacksmith loaned a sledge hammer, bang — bang — bang — and back on the road. The tank now fitted on the bonnet is a recent modification. It was decided to use the car in a tableau for a huge torchlight procession marking the recent Coronation celebrations, but examination showed a leak on the tap to the petrol tank which, unfortunately, could not be quickly remedied, so an emergency, gravity-fed tank was fitted on the bonnet and like Tennyson's brook — the old bus just kept on running, a real tribute to the workmanship and design of yesterday.

The outline details of a 5,000-mile trip, within 200 miles of the Arctic Circle, in a 1926 model 7 h.p. Jowett Car was submitted by H. J. Summers, 22, Victoria Road, Padiham, Lancs.

A 5,000-mile trip, within 200 miles of the Arctic Circle, including an excursion almost to the summit of Galdhoppiggen (8,021 ft.) (Norway), having traversed roads in Sweden which consisted of tree trunks laid in swampland, would be a test for any car, but when it is made in a 1926 model 7 h.p. Jowett, then it ranks as a TRIP.

In June, 1949, Mr. T. Bracewell, then an undergraduate at Cambridge University, left Clayton-le-Moors, near Accrington, on a journey that took him first to Folkestone — Calais — Bruges — Brussels — Liege — Spa — Dusseldorf — Hamelin — Travern-mundo — Nilarg — Copenhagen — Helsingborg — Stockholm — and then up into Jamtland, where he took part in an elk hunt only 200 miles south of the Arctic Circle.

His return was via Metadelan, a small, Norwegian village, where he climbed to within sight of the summit of Galdhoppiggen in his little car, then ploughing through bright snow over the mountain route to Oslo. From there to Frederikshavn — Bremen — into Holland, via the Hook to Harwich, and then home.

Apart from one accident, his total

ARCTIC CIRCLE

The next four pictures relate to another heroic restoration, this time of a 1926 Short-Two. Above is a copy of a *Mechanix Illustrated* article dated 1954, which gives details of how a student bought the car from a scrap yard and who then took it on a 5,000 mile trip almost to the Arctic Circle.

The next two pictures show the car in 1960 when it was rescued by Fred Barrett. By that time the car had been heavily vandalised. The car was stored for years and the building it was in collapsed in 1967, burying it in rubble. The car had to be dismantled to get it out of its tomb and was then stored in its dismantled state until 1969. Fred then restored the car which took over 1,000 man-hours of work to complete.

The History of the 1926 Short-Two registered CB 6682, Richard Gane, January 2012

The car was purchased new on 9 October 1926 from Tom Beach's, Park Garage, Brownhill, Blackburn, by a Mr Wilding, who at the time was chief Motor Tax officer at Blackburn. He was able to verify the car's authenticity after the restoration. The car lived and was used locally until 1939 when records show that it was scrapped. Its whereabouts during the war years remain a mystery but it was found in a scrap yard in Clayton-le-Moors near Accrington in 1949 (see period article below). A University student bought it for £15 and almost immediately, drove it through Europe to Scandinavia and into the Arctic Circle on a study of continental agricultural methods. The return journey was over 5,000 miles.

In 1960, it was found by F. Barrett of Accrington at the rear of the student's house in a deplorable state, having been vandalised and suffering from eleven years exposure to the weather. The car was brought inside and stored but in 1967 the building it was in collapsed during a gale and the Jowett was buried under tons of rubble. A large roof truss kept most of the rubble off the car but it was necessary to dig down and dismantle the car to remove it piece by piece. The Jowett was then stored again, this time in bits, until February 1969, when restoration commenced.

The car was stripped to the last nut and bolt and over 1,000 man-hours were put into restoring the vehicle. For the radiator alone, 5,500 gills were stamped out and then soldered onto the tubes one at a time. The car first ran on the road again in May 1970. In June that year it successfully completed the 160-mile Manchester to Blackpool run.

The Observer, Saturday 22 October 1949

A 23-year-old car bought for £15 by Mr Tom Bracewell, a student at Cambridge University of 48 Burnley Road, Clayton-le-Moors has completed a journey of 5,000 miles through Belgium, Germany, Denmark, Sweden, Norway and Holland.

Mr Bracewell last year hitch-hiked to the South of Italy and back starting from the lights at the Load of Mischief. This year he particularly wanted to visit Scandinavia. He has taken his degree at Cambridge, but he is staying on for a further year to take a diploma in estate management and forestry. He felt he needed to study the Scandinavian methods at first hand. Two or three weeks before setting out he bought the car from Mr Threlfall of Henry Street, Clayton-le-Moors.

Mr Bracewell set out on his journey on the Monday of Accrington Holiday Week. He had previously been in contact with Jowett's, the makers of the car. The engine was in order, but the firm overhauled the brakes and transmission. He had some difficulty in insuring the car but eventually he found a firm willing to undertake the job. Mr Bracewell also bought two new tyres but did not put them on. He only had two punctures. The Jowett firm informed their agents on the Continent, and on several occasions, thanks to that agreement, Mr Bracewell was able to complete a remarkable trip. On one day he covered 100 miles and never saw another car. In Norway he took the car over roads over the mountains. He went up over Goldhopiggen (2,468 metres) – the highest mountain in Scandinavia to within sight of the summit. In parts of Sweden some roads were merely tree trunks laid across the swamp.

The most serious accident he encountered was in Germany on the way home. There was a road diversion on the Autobahn. It was night and he did not see the notice – which was in German anyhow. The car ended in a vertical position in a pile of asphalt. The back axle was bent. And was roughly repaired with the use of a sledge hammer in a nearby garage. The axle was out of alignment with the front wheels and although the car ran it resulted in great wear on the tyres and time and money were low. Nevertheless he managed to pull through.

Apart from the motoring side the holiday had other adventures. In Sweden, learning that elk hunting was coming on, he got a job during the corn harvest in order that he could stay on for the elk hunting. He saw the way the Swedes gather their corn and dry it in racks following methods quite different from those in this country.

Finally he set off with a party of twenty-five Swedes for the elk hunting; only one spoke a little English. They took food for four days and went 20 kilometres into the forest. Antlers which Mr Bracewell has brought home are unfortunately not the ones from the elk he shot. Dogs made off with the body while it was dried. The antlers are to be sent on to him if they can be found.

With a tent stowed in the back of the car, he never had to worry about lodgings, but often in Sweden people would come up to him and told him it was too cold to sleep out and offered him lodgings for the night. He went within 200 miles of the Artic Circle.

Some of his worst adventures were on the way home. At the German frontier it was found that his military permit had expired, and while hunting in Sweden he had failed to notice it. The customs officials threatened to send him back to Copenhagen. He responded by threatening to ring up Mr Bevan. Finally they let him through on the proviso that he crossed Germany in a day. His accident on the Autobahn prevented that. At the first frontier post into Holland at the other side the officials refused to let him through. He tried another, and the officials there were extremely arrogant and demanded to see the money. He could only show them a £1 note, and while he searched round the car pretending to find the rest, the man lectured him about the currency. In doing so he completely forgot to look at the date on the passport and let him through.

Making for the Hook of Holland, he saw a notice, 'To the boats', but ended up at a sailing lake instead of the Channel steamers. The result of this was that he arrived at the boat as the people were all waving 'Good bye'.

Very much against their will he persuaded the men at the dockside to work their crane and lift the car on board. He then discovered he had no ticket and no money to pay for one. The man at the booking office refused to take a cheque, "But my car is on the ship" he pleaded. Finally they agreed to let him go and the RAC forwarded a cheque from this side for him. Not only was he anxious to get home because his money was finished, but it was also necessary to get back to Cambridge.

'And what are you going to do with the car now?' an *Observer* reporter asked Mr Bracewell. 'It is going for export to help Britain's recovery,' he replied. 'A man in Denmark wants to buy it, I've told him that it's worth £300 to me, and it really is worth that – It's done jolly well.'

I am not sure what happened to the car after this article was written in October 1949, but it clearly was not exported to Denmark, as the restored car was featured on the front cover of *The Jowetteer* dated June 1987. At that time it gave details of how Fred Barrett found the car and restored it.

Fred Barrett's car was the subject of the press cutting featured above. The car actually got to within twenty miles of the Arctic Circle and it was the front axle that was damaged. (The article was incorrect saying it was the rear axle that was damaged. N.S.) The plate welded on in Germany is still there. Fred discovered the car in a deplorable state in 1961, as it had been abandoned in a field behind the owner's house and vandals had smashed everything breakable. Fred and his son restored the car over a nine-year period and it finally took to the road in 1970.

The restored car is now owned by Richard Gane and is seen regularly at Club rallies and events. It is seen here in all its glory in the hotel foyer at our National Rally in Daventry in 2011.

Probably the two most famous Jowett cars built were 'Wait & See' which were produced in 1926 and no history of Jowett, however small, would be complete without a reference to them. In 1926, Frank Gray, the former MP for Oxford must have been a Godsend to Jowett Cars, as he had been complaining that British cars were not suitable for Colonial use. He challenged the British Motor Industry to provide him with cars which would be capable of crossing Africa, carrying all their own petrol, water and provisions, as most of the journey would have to be covered without any outside help. This was due to the fact that there were virtually no roads or services in Africa at that time. Needless to say there were no offers forthcoming from other car manufacturers as such a trip had never been attempted before. The Jowett brothers, however, realised the free advertising potential such a trip would create and agreed to sell Gray two cars. Being two shrewd Yorkshiremen, they said they would repay Gray the cost of the two cars if the trip was successful, this way Gray would also have a financial interest in completing the challenge! Prior to the trip a reporter asked Ben Jowett if the cars had any real chance of completing such an arduous journey, he replied 'Wait and See'. Gladney Haigh heard this and ordered the two cars to be sign-written on each side one 'Wait' and the other 'See', and the rest is history! These are the cars at the factory prior to departure to Africa. (Jowett Car Club Archive)

Preparing to leave Umkedada, British Sudan. (Jowett Car Club Archive)

Repair work on the cars start outside Am Dam. (Jowett Car Club Archive)

Top: One incredible situation Gray and Sawyer found themselves in was when a shackled slave-woman came up to them to ask for help to get away from her captors. Needless to say, they were up to the challenge and released her from her ankle chains and took her well over a hundred miles out of their way to the police at Umkedada and safety. She is clearly visible in the back of 'Wait' in this picture. (Jowett Car Club Archive)

Middle: This is what Gray and Sawyer called a 'good' type of road! (Jowett Car Club Archive)

Bottom: The car's triumphant return to Bradford. At the centre of the picture is Bismark, the African mechanic/guide, who accompanied Gray and Sawyer for the whole journey across Africa. He had said he would assist with the trip providing Gray agreed to bring him back to England after the crossing. Clearly, Gray was a man of his word as Bismark travelled with the cars as they were displayed at Jowett agencies all over the country. (Jowett Car Club Archive)

During the 1920s, Jowett Cars produced charming olive-coloured little booklets, the same size as the Handbook, called *Opinions of Jowett Owners*. These booklets seemed to be published every few months, as the first copy I have is the 5th Edition, which was published in 1924 and the last one I have is the 11th Edition, which is dated March 1929. They all say that the original letters can be inspected at the works, and that:

> Our greatest trouble is in selecting a number of letters to make the most varied appeal. If there is any point upon which you would like the opinion of past users of our cars, we shall be glad to send you copies of appropriate letters on the subject.
>
> We have divided the letters under three headings, viz :- General, Overseas & Commercial

I think that this could be a bit of poetic licence as a good number of these testimonials are repeated in several of the editions, but they are great fun nonetheless! The following are a small selection of them:

Extraordinary Performance under Appalling Conditions

The letter as under was received from Mr Galton-Fenzie, the Honorary Secretary of the Royal East African Automobile Association at the conclusion of a SIX MONTHS' TEST of a Jowett four-seater car in East Africa.

> The Jowett has now completed 6,000 miles, and has been on the road since August, i.e., for a period of six months. It covered 1,350 miles in Kenya over appalling roads, with a load of three people and about 300lbs. of luggage. During this trip, only oil, petrol and a cupful of water were added, and in spite of this gruelling time, it came through the ordeal untouched. It was then sent up to Uganda in October, where it completed the rest of the 6,000 miles. This part of the test was, to my mind, unnecessarily severe, as the car was driven by some eighteen people, some of whom had never driven a car before, and learnt on the Jowett. Besides covering very nearly the whole of Uganda by road, some indifferent, and some bad, the Jowett was driven with a full load cross-country where the going was so bad and the track so narrow that no other car had ever attempted the journey. Although the Jowett was not built or ever meant for this rough work, it not only accomplished all that was asked of it in a most satisfactory manner, but throughout the trial it had no mechanical breakdown whatsoever, which speaks volumes for the material used, and the workmanship of the Jowett Car Company. It had one accident, owing to its being left outside a house in Kampala on a steep hill. During the night the car took charge, and after about 300 yards run knocked down the front steps and most of the verandah of another house; the only damage to the car was a burst front tyre and a slightly bent front axle, which was easily straightened.
>
> The valves have been ground in once, and it has not yet been necessary to decarbonise the engine. The power developed by this little 7hp engine is nothing short of marvellous, as it has often taken a full load of for people and luggage, etc, long distances over bad

roads, and averaged 25-30 miles an hour. The best driving speed was 30 to 35mph, and under favourable conditions it can touch 60 miles an hour. As to hill climbing, it is guaranteed to take a full load up a gradient of 1 in 2½, and the petrol consumption varies from 35-50 miles to the gallon, according to the conditions. Everyone who has driven or ridden in the Jowett expressed their amazement and wonder at the extraordinary performance which this little car puts up, the low running cost, and the exceptional strength of the chassis. The only criticisms put forward have been that the tyres were too small, the steering very light, and the body flimsy-looking. In actual practice, however, except for the tyres, which could be larger, everything has stood up extraordinary well. I personally thought that it was very short-sighted on the part of the manufacturers not to send out any parts with the car, but their optimism was justified, as not a single part had to be replaced or repaired, in spite of the severity of the test, which took more out of the car in six months than the average driver takes in two years.

Dear Sir,

I have much pleasure in furnishing you with a testimonial regarding the performance of my Jowett car.

It was purchased direct from the manufacturers prior to an agent being appointed in the North Island, and it arrived in the Dominion eighteen months ago.

I might here mention that previous to its arrival I was told many times of my folly in purchasing a car with only a twin cylinder engine, which, it was stated, would be absolutely useless on New Zealand.

However, since the car has arrived, I have travelled over 12,000, practically all of which have been done over the Waitomo, Taumarunui, Ohura and Whagamomona country roads.

Those who know these roads will, I think, agree with me when I say they are some of, if not the very, worst in New Zealand.

The long steep grades that are encountered on these back country roads the Jowett has climbed with ease, and I have travelled thousands of miles over mud roads which have in many cases been axle deep.

I do not think that any other make of car has been put to a more gruelling test, and yet, after travelling these 12,000 miles the engine is running better than ever, and the body does not show any sign of strain, nor has it developed the slightest rattle.

I have had only three punctures, and the original tyres are still on and good for another hundred miles.

The water in the radiator has boiled once, but this was no fault of the engine, and was caused by my ignorance.

I have never once been prevented from reaching my destination through engine trouble or other cause whatsoever.

On metal roads I can travel in perfect comfort whatever the weather and maintain an average speed of 25 to 30 miles an hour.

If you should have any prospective purchasers who are still doubtful as to the power of the little engine, just send them to me and I will convince them in a few hours that the Jowett will do all that is claimed of it, and more.

In conclusion I have no hesitation in asserting that there is no car as good as a British car, and no British car as good as the Jowett.

I am a satisfied Jowett owner.

H. V. Chatterton, 14 June 1926

GIBRALTAR

Dear Sirs,

After doing a trip to Palamos (Gerona), about 180 kilometres beyond Barcelona, and back to Gibraltar on a Jowett full four-seater, without having had the very slightest of trouble, I feel I must write and tell you what I think about your cars.

They are incomparable, trustworthy, and of the toughest quality. I left Gibraltar on the 23rd with a most heavy load on board. My wife and myself weigh just on 200 kilos; my two sons weigh just over 170 kilos between them; then I carried two very bulky suitcases. I also took two boxes full of marine engine catalogues for propaganda purposes. I also carried 87 kilos of tools. I went to Palamos to install two 36hp marine engines, so had to take all my boring tackle and full equipment of tools with which to install these engines. When I left Gibraltar it was a very windy day and I had to firmly lash up the hood so as to prevent it torn in the wind.

We left Gibraltar at 9 a.m., stopped at Vejer de la Frontera over one and a half hours , then carried on to Jerez de la Frontera, and then on to Seville, arriving there at 4.30 p.m.; we had dinner, and left at 6.15 p.m. for Almendralejos, but finding no accommodation there we carried on to Merida, arriving there half an hour before midnight. The whole of this trip was done in pouring rain.

We stopped at Madrid two days, then left at 9 a.m. for Zaragoza, which we reached at 5.30 p.m. after losing 3½ hours over taking meals and taking in fuel.

The most wonderful thing about this trip was that we did not have a single puncture on the whole trip. We came across some awful roads, and, as it was raining so heavily, we constantly came across deep pools and streams.

I would recommend some of your people at home who think they are doing big things to come out here and try some of these roads, then they will see the meaning of rough roads.

Now comes the most wonderful part of the whole performance. We averaged the whole way a consumption of 6 litres to every 100 kilometres (47mpg). The extremely low cost of this trip was almost unbelievable. Nothing about the car suffered in the slightest, and the only trouble we had was to garage the car at the end of the day's trip and having to fill up with fuel and occasionally having to pour oil into the crank-chamber.

The day after arriving in Gibraltar my son went down to Barbate (about 100 kilometres way from Gibraltar). He was away at Barbate eight days, and during this time he had to make two return trips every day to Veiger de la Frontera, or say 40 kilos daily, and all this running about without having touched the car after its return from Palamos.

I am ready at any time to run in competition with any car that anybody wishes to run with on a long trip such as I did, with the condition that they must do the same as I did, i.e., do a complete trip without touching the car or engine or tyres.

The Jowett is the most wonderful car I have ever seen. I shall not rest until I have proved all I say. Also I shall not rest until I have one of your saloon cars. Please let me know the exact cost of a saloon car delivered to Gibraltar. I assure you that once people realise the enormous value of your cars, your car will make itself immensely popular.

It is a great pity that English people are so slow to find out that they have the best in their own country.

Please accept my best thanks for having sent me such a fine and trustworthy car. You cannot imagine my feelings when the car was brought to the hotel door every time we left a town; on seeing the car we felt we were always near home; the car was really at home.

I wish I could find the proper words with which to express my admiration of this good and tried friend. May you manufacture and sell the largest number of cars in England soon.

Yours sincerely,

Thomas A. Smith, 1 December 1926

BATAVIA

Dear Sirs,

Having now driven my Jowett full four-seater, which you shipped over to me to Java at the end of last year, for a period of seven months, in which time I have covered a distance of 4,500 miles, I should like to write to you to telling you how very satisfied indeed I am with the car.

In this country 90 per cent of cars are of American origin, and my former experience was with American cars, cheap ones and medium priced ones. Compared with these cars the Jowett scores in the following points:-

1) Economy – The running costs of the cheapest car to run I formerly owned were exactly twice as high as the running costs of a Jowett. I do 50 miles per gallon regularly.

2) Ease of upkeep – Owing to the simple lay-out and construction of the Jowett you need not be an engineer to keep the car in tune.

3) Vibration-less and smooth running.

4) Silence at road speeds exceeding 25 miles per hour.

5) Roominess – I am 6 feet 3 inches tall, but the leg room in the driver's seat is ample.

6) Suspension and road-holding capabilities – The Jowett holds the poor roads in this country as steady as a rock right up to her maximum speed of 43mph. Whether I am alone or with a full load the suspension, aided by balloon tyres and Smith shock absorbers, is excellent; there is no swaying or bouncing, and corners can be taken extremely fast.

7) Freedom from overheating – I have been driving the car all day for a distance of 200 miles and there was no necessity to add water during or at the end of the day. I have been driving for one hour and a half at 35mph, the temperature being 90 degrees in the shade, and it was a sunny road all the time and then up a hill which asks for

ten minutes full throttle in second gear for ten miles in succession, and have climbed gradients of 1 in 4 with a full load up to a height of 5,000 feet above sea level in first gear but have never boiled. I admit that American cars are a little faster on the hills which they can rush up in top gear, but on long hills of a winding nature they will always start boiling and lose much time in filling up with water.

To conclude, I have had none of the minor but irritating troubles that other cheap cars will develop within the first 2,000 miles. I have covered about 1,500 miles up country through and up the mountains on roads which in a distance of 20 miles cause one to have to negotiate as many as 250 hair-pin corners and sharp bends without feeling tired after a drive of 150 miles or more in one day. On a trip of 120 miles, during which I climbed to 3,000 feet, dropped again to 1,500 feet, climbed again to 3,500 feet, dropped once more to 2,000 feet, and eventually ended at 2,500 feet above sea level, I averaged 25mph easily. Other cars may be able to do better, but not on 50mpg. I can assure you that I am not only thoroughly satisfied and delighted with the car, but also proud of it. Formerly I was always wanting something different than what I had just owned, generally a more expensive car which I could not afford. The Jowett has put an end to this feeling; I just want a Jowett and nothing else.
Yours faithfully,
O. Sielcken, 3 August 1926

Cape Town, SOUTH AFRICA
Dear Sirs,
I am compelled, through sheer enthusiasm born of complete satisfaction with the excellent performance of my Jowett (bought in February last year), to add my quota of praise to the extraordinary merits of your cars, as exemplified by the day-in and day-out running in all sorts of weather; in a word, the little car is a wonder, and nobody can believe what she is capable of doing unless they actually become a passenger, whether in hustling city traffic or flying over the open 'Veld' at a cruising speed from 30 to 35 miles per hour.

It may interest you to know, and for the benefit of some doubting Thomas's, that although I have owned five British, five American and one German car, I have come to the conclusion that the little Jowett beats them all for practical, utility, dependability, economy and freedom of trouble. The original tyres have done over 17,000 miles and look good for another 10,000 miles at least. The engine has been decarbonised twice, and the repairs account is a negligible quantity.

The 'Home' people must recognise that a car has to stand up to much harder work here in the Union of South Africa than in the 'Old Country'; all the same, nothing daunts the ubiquitous Jowett, which is a trusty and loveable little bus, no matter what the weather or roads have to be negotiated. Her appetite is, as they say, that of a canary, whilst her pull is that of an elephant, with a petrol consumption of 45 to 50 miles per gallon, according to the nature of roads and stoppages.

I can only endorse the sentiments of Captain James' letter of September 8 in the *Light Car* of September 16, when he says of all his cars: 'I have never had one to touch the JOWETT.' I might add that my personal regret is that there are not more of them in this country, as the Jowett is without doubt the car par excellence for the conditions pertaining throughout this vast continent, and, to crown all, the Jowett neither boils or bucks, which is saying a great deal, considering the varying climatic altitudes we have.

I may state that I hope to start a Jowett Club here before very long, and in the meantime this communication is addressed to you to make what use you like of it to further the interests of the manufacturers of this unique light car.

Yours faithfully,

W. T. Forsyth, 27 October 1927

District Lyallpur

PUNJAB, India

Dear Sirs,

I purchased a Jowett four-seater car just out of England in October 1927, for our district work.

I think you would like to know that we are delighted with her; she has done 37 miles to the gallon over the most appalling unmade roads, has been through deep sand, water and mud without turning a hair.

The 8½ inch clearance is a great boon over our bad roads, which are full of deep ruts, and the lightness is a great boon where the mud or sand is deep, as we can extract her so easily without calling for assistance.

I had a ------ four-seater before the Jowett, but I infinitely prefer the Jowett.

I enclose a snapshot of her taken outside one of our Punjabi villages, to one of which she goes to almost daily.

I think you may appreciate this unsolicited testimony.

Miss D. M. Orton, 25 July 1928

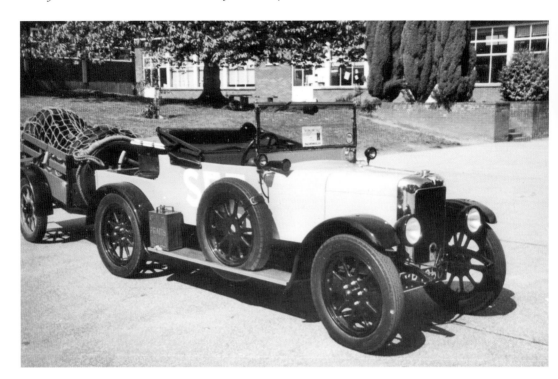

This is the 1926 'See'. It is an exact copy of the original car, and some think it is the actual car, but in any event, it is correct in every detail even down to the restored Eccles trailer it is pulling. The car was the subject of a heroic restoration which fills me with admiration.

Long-Two re-built as SE. Mike Eames, May 2002

This car was first purchased unregistered but as 'used' in July 1926 and was registered as YP 1950. The car was used until 1929 when it went off the road after a major breakdown of mechanical components. Excessive wear was found throughout the car and the owner apparently then entered into a protracted and unsuccessful warranty claim against the Jowett Car Company.

We are told that the owner, who resided in Southborough, Kent, stored the car in the basement garage of a relative, near to his home, and sometime after his death in the late thirties it remained there. We understand that this property was destroyed during a bombing raid in the early part of the Second World War and that in view of the fact that there had been no human casualties were involved and that the devastation was complete down to ground level, the site was leveled and the remains of the car were entombed.

This bombsite became a car park and it was not until the mid- to late eighties that redevelopment caused the Jowett to be unearthed. The hand of chance now presents itself in this story, for a neighbour of the original owner was contacted and he, in turn, contacted two people – the husband of the original owner's daughter, and Fred Barrett who already owned a Jowett Short-Two. The exhumed remains, together with the original registration documentation were taken to Fred's home in Accrington, where it resided more or less undisturbed until mid- to late 2001. (Fred, had in fact, started work on some of the components, but most of his time and attention had been taken up with the Short-Two).

A chance telephone call, in response to some advertised literature that Fred was selling, set about a chain of events which resulted in this car coming out of slumber and moving on to a new home. In view of the fact that there are a number of good examples of this marque in existence, and as a tribute to the pioneering spirit of our forefathers, it was decided to recreate *See* of 'Wait and See' fame (the reason behind the decision – *Wait* was known to have been scrapped and *See* was refurbished and sold on after its epic journey). Again fate takes a hand because after examining this car in close detail prior to any work being undertaken, it was found to have quite extreme wear throughout its construction, and the rear chassis had additional drillings not normally found in a production model. Fred was advised of our intentions and his only comment being, 'funny you should think that, but I thought of *See* when I first saw the vehicle.' Is somebody trying to tell us something? – We will never know.

The body was reconstructed using the original parts where possible and the rear section fabricated using the original Jowett designs and was returned to the road after its long slumber in time for the 2002 National Rally.

A rear view of a blue and black 1926 Short-Two showing the dickey seat open. The dickey seat could comfortably accommodate two children, but it would be a very snug fit for two adults!

This is a Jowett advertising shot of a 1926 Chummy. Attractive models were often hired to put a bit of glamour into the pictures, and the young lady in the passenger seat is almost certainly one of them. I like this atmospheric picture as, not only does it feature the car well, but it also shows how farming has moved on since then. The corn field behind is not full of plastic rolls filled with straw, but shows stooks of corn drying before collection by the farmer. (Jowett Car Club Archive)

Advertising Jowett Cars

I have always been fascinated by Jowett advertising, as in my opinion, it had a style all of its own. This began at the start of Jowett car production in the early 1920s and remained basically the same right up to the Second World War.

When the Jowett brothers moved to the new purpose-built factory at Five Lane Ends at Idle, it enabled car manufacture to commence again by April 1920. At this time the Jowett brothers took on more clerical staff and increased the workforce. Two important appointments in respect of publicity and advertising took place at this time; the first was Harry Mitchell, who started as works manager. At the time of his appointment he had been working for ABC Motor Cycles Ltd. He was a very sociable person and produced Jowett adverts and sales brochures and arranged publicity events. The second appointment was Gladney Haigh who came in from a Bradford garage selling Karrier commercial vehicles. He was appointed as a buyer but in 1927 he took over writing sales booklets and adverts after Harry Mitchell left the company.

From the very start of their advertising the main theme was to extol the fact that the cars were sturdy and strong and, above all, cheap to run and maintain. The style in which this was done was unique as far as I am concerned, as many adverts never pictured the cars at all but were full of poetic prose, asking the reader to send for a sales brochure. Another popular theme was to wax lyrical about the virtues of Yorkshire, and if possible, make fun of Lancashire at the same time! I think it would be fair to say that it was Harry Mitchell who started this wonderful style, but was carried on to great effect from 1927 by Gladney Haigh.

It was as early as 1923 when one of Jowett's best-known slogans was first penned, 'The little engine with the big pull'; this of course was the first of many.

Some advertising slogans taken from the 1920s Jowett Light Car 7/17hp Instruction Book

The Jowett slogan – 'The little engine with the big pull' – is so apt and characteristic of the car that it has become known throughout the British Empire. We also append a number of other slogans and complementary descriptions which have been applied to our cars from time to time.

The car that is designed to last a lifetime – and does.

Jowetts never wear out – they're left to the next of kin.

If you want to go where a Jowett won't, you'll need a crane.

You cannot motor for less than it costs on a Jowett, unless you are always a guest.

The Jowett has the pull of an elephant, the appetite of a canary; and the docility of a lamb.

Where there's a way a Jowett will go – easily!

The Jowett made luxury motoring economical.

The seven that passes a seventeen like a seventy.

Makes milestones s'milestones.

'Try not the pass', the old man said, until he saw the car was a Jowett; then he asked for a lift – and got it!

Carries the whole family at the rail fare of one.

MARCH 21, 1924　　THE LIGHT CAR AND CYCLECAR　　15

ON ILKLA' MOOR B'ART 'AT.

Cow and Calf Rocks, Ilkley.

Our caption is a bit of real
"Yorkshire."

So also is the Jowett Car.

"Kuklos" says it contains "all
the best of Yorkshire except
the pudding."

"The little engine with the big
pull" goes everywhere.

2-Seater,　　　　　　　　4-Seater,
One-sixty-eight.　　　　　One-ninety-two.

JOWETT CARS Ltd., Idle, BRADFORD.

The Jowett
" The little engine with the big pull "

1923 PROGRAMME

THREE MODELS

2-Seater	£220

Complete with all-weather curtains, solid nickel radiator, and full equipment.

2-Seater	£225

As above, with double dickey seat.

4-Seater	£245

Complete with all-weather curtains, solid nickel radiator, and full equipment, 8' 6" wheelbase, and same generous leg room as in 2-seater model.

Self-Starter on all Models £15 extra

RECENT SUCCESSES. SUNDERLAND and District Motor Club Trial, held Aug. 27: SILVER CUP won outright by R. Scoon, driving a JOWETT. SCOTTISH TWO DAYS Edinburgh and District Motor Club, Sept. 14: GOLD MEDAL awarded to Major Johnstone driving a JOWETT CAR. Also member of team winning CLUB CUP.

NO FURTHER REDUCTIONS

ORDERS can be placed immediately for new JOWETT Models, our 1923 policy being definitely defined by particulars above.

The popular demand for a four-seater car as good as the JOWETT Two-Seater has led to the introduction of the New Four-Seater Model, which is fitted with the same sturdy engine which has put up so many remarkable performances in the most arduous Reliability Trials of recent years. Any JOWETT Agent will be pleased to give you a demonstration of its qualities. May we put you in touch?

JOWETT CARS, LTD.
Dept. F. IDLE, BRADFORD

STAND 61 WHITE CITY.

LIVE AGENTS for 1923 are required.

7 h.p. JOWETT Two-Seater with Dickey.

THE AUTOCAR.   ADVERTISEMENTS.   JANUARY 22ND, 1926.   9

"FAMILY COACH"

Baby Brown opened the door for Mrs. Brown, who was driven by Johnny Brown: meanwhile Mr. Brown, surveyed with evident pride, the Brown family coach, which happened to be blue.

We have all played the game "Family Coach," and how we roared when the bottom fell out!

No need to fear this in a Jowett Coach, because everything "Jowett" is well made.

We *knocked* the bottom out of coach costs with this unique model, costing only £200, complete with 6 lamps, Starter and Dunlop Balloon Tyres. Upholstered in Bedford Cord.

You can have a fully licensed and insured Jowett for £35 down and 28/- weekly for 2 years. May we send you D-P folder and catalogue?

JOWETT CARS, IDLE, BRADFORD

THE AUTOCAR.   *ADVERTISEMENTS.*   SEPTEMBER 21ST, 1923.   13

Let's go on our own to day

SOMETIMES mere man is de trop — after he has purchased the car. Here we depict one such occasion. You will of course note that the ladies are clad in spotless white. They know their Jowett is a no trouble car, and keeps clean inside and out. The accessibility of the controls is exemplified in the lower picture. Gear, brake and ignition being within easy reach of the driver's right hand. And the price is within easy reach of the man of moderate means.

£168 completely equipped with framed side curtains, 5 Dunlop wheels and cord tyres, and speedometer. There are no extras unless you desire a starter, which costs £10.

Write to-day for the literature that is different to Dept. E.

JOWETT CARS LTD., IDLE, BRADFORD.

15-16   MENTION OF "THE AUTOCAR," WHEN WRITING TO ADVERTISERS, WILL ENSURE PROMPT ATTENTION.   A13

Chance, or Thought

When you sit in the front or back seat of a Jowett, and stretch your length restfully, we hope you don't think it is merely a matter of luck that there is such a large amount of leg-room.

The special design of our engine helps, of course, but there has been a tremendous amount of planning for your comfort.

The same with the upholstery and trimming.

It's the same the whole way through.

When your left hand seeks the gear lever, there is no groping to do, it is there, naturally. Likewise, your right hand falls on the brake lever.

We can give you a reason for everything except one.

We can't explain why our seven horse engine pulls a twelve horse body with ease, and further, passes most cars of higher power.

To prove what we say, you ought to try a Jowett, and you can, for nothing.

Prices from £150.   Tax £7.

JOWETT CARS LTD., IDLE, BRADFORD

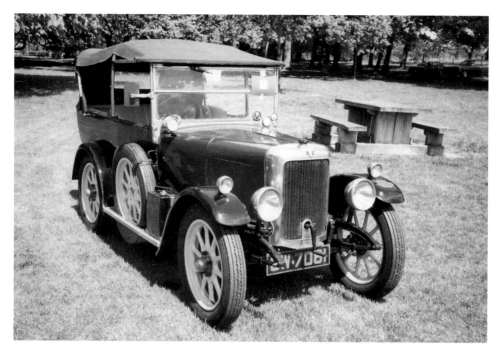

This is the 1926 Light-Four (Chummy) as purchased by the club's Pre-War Registrar, Ian Priestley, in 1988 in its green and yellow livery.

The same car as it is today in its grey and black livery after a full restoration by Ian Priestley. (Priestley)

These charming period pictures show a *c.* 1926 Short-Four model (the Chummy). It shows its proud owner having a smoke on his pipe before setting off again on his journey. I found these pictures on a website called www.oldclassiccar. co.uk which is run by Richard Jones. This is a fantastic website, which as can be gleaned from the title, is a classic car enthusiast's paradise, I am most grateful to Richard for allowing me to use these pictures in this book.

This is a modern survivor of a 1926 Light-Four (Chummy) this example is in the Shuttleworth Collection in Biggleswade, Bedfordshire. Richard Shuttleworth is best known for his involvement with aeroplanes and Brooklands race track. He did, however, have three Jowetts himself including a 'Chummy', which he used to drive to various locations around the Brooklands track. He sold one of his Jowetts to Bill Boddy, the legendary editor of the *Motor Sport* magazine.

Richard Shuttleworth – The Shuttleworth Collection

A 1926 Jowett Light-Four (Chummy) is one of the cars on display at the Shuttleworth Collection in Biggleswade, Bedfordshire.

In the book, *Richard Shuttleworth – An illustrated biography* by Kevin Desmond, I was rather hoping Richard may have been pictured in one of his Jowetts, but alas no. He did quote some remarks made by Charles Martin, which I found very amusing, so I am reproducing them here.

To continuously commute to and fro on his estate and elsewhere, Richard was a tremendous devotee of the flat-twin cylinder Jowett open tourers. Charles Martin explains:

You've never met a Jowett, have you? Oh Jesus! They were built at the side of a house in Idle, Bradford, to go over the Yorkshire Moors. There was a four-seater model and a two-seater model. The two-seater was 8 feet long and 4 feet high, you could almost pick it up and turn it round like a pram – I kid you not. It's worth trying to find one to have a look at it. Maximum speed was 45mph from a three speed cogbox and the bottom gear was low enough to travel at 5mph.

Now Richard was besotted with these, owned one long-chassis and two short-chassis Jowetts. You can take them anywhere. I can forget about them and come back to them, and if one of them won't go, I can take bits off the other to make it go. He was the only person I have ever known to enter the Paddock at Brooklands and use the revs of the Jowett to play out the tune of the National Anthem!"

He was also heard to remark, 'A Jowett is the only car I know that will go across a field of Brussels sprouts in top gear!'

Side view of the Shuttleworth Collection's 1926 Light-Four (Chummy) (The Shuttleworth Collection)

Instrumentation on the dash board was very sparse in the 1920s! (The Shuttleworth Collection)

This Freedom

"Man is free, the moment he wishes to be."
Voltaire

T H I S F R E E D O M

HAVING now dealt with the general features of all our cars, let us lead you, gently, towards the mechanical side. Having inspected all on deck, we descend into the engine-room. Mechanism is much less interesting than, but equally as important as, the poetry of motoring. On the other hand, we have left it until the later pages of this book because the general excellence of our chassis work is so well known to all those experienced in these matters. Jowett performance on hills, after nearly two decades, is still a wonder to the world, and the following pages will give you all the information you need regarding the engine and chassis. You cannot afford to miss the opportunity of a trial run in a Jowett Car. It is most convincing. Any Agent will arrange this on request.

T H I S   F R E E D O M

THIS is a picture of a Jowett in Equatorial Africa. Think of the hottest day you ever knew in England ; think of the cars that pass you—boiling. Imagine these cars struggling over tracks like this but in a temperature 30° higher. How long would they stick it, do you think—and how much water would they need if they survived ? The Jowett only required water at the rate of 5,000 miles to the gallon. We also publish a folder describing a journey of many hundreds of miles into the desert from Alexandria. It is a joy to read it, and realise how the Jowett negotiates appalling country —easily. We have multitudes of records of similar feats. A Jowett is invincible Overseas. There are reasons for this invincibility ! Sturdy design is not the least, but correct design is the most important.

THESE FACTS ARE SIGNIFICANT

AVERAGE 4-SEATER	JOWETT 4-SEATER
The average 4-seater weighs a ton, and with adult passengers gives a loading of 6½ cwts. per wheel.	The Jowett 4-seater weighs 10½ cwts., with adult passengers gives a wheel loading of only 4 cwts. approximately.

The more you think about such facts the greater is your realisation that the Jowett is right because it is made *right.*

THIS FREEDOM

NO idle drumming of impatient hands on the window pane, with a luring dream of green fields and running brooks. It's "Pack up the luncheon basket; get ready, everyone! Rain, rain go away. That silver lining to the cloud spells sunshine yonder, over the hills. We're off!" And so out you go, any day—winter or summer—rain or shine. Such freedom! You can use your Jowett Saloon on 366 days (leap year).

We like the lines of our saloon, the handsome taut trim look of her, the true beauty of perfect utility—a Frigate of the free highway. But hidden beneath those lines there is the cosiest accommodation you ever dreamed possible on a road carriage. Big, deep, delightfully sprung seats, and pillowy seat-backs, finished and trimmed in a way worthy of a boudoir, but in tough, serviceable, deep-ribbed Bedford cord.

Windows that give the interior as much light (and air if you want it) as in an open car, high enough to let the passengers see all the country on each side of the car. The view in most saloons is restricted to one side only. Yes, civilisation on wheels!

Seventeen

This is a 1927 Short-Four or 'Chummy'. This model was first introduced in 1925 and proved to be a very popular model.

This is a 1927 Saloon, known as a 'Greenhouse' saloon due to the large amount of window space. The saloon was first introduced in 1926 and was available with a fabric body or in aluminium. This car is owned by Mike Koch-Osborne, the grandson of William Jowett. This picture shows the 'as found' condition of the car when Mike bought it after its very long slumber.

This is the same car today after its full restoration by Mike last year, details of which appear in the 'Owner's of today' section of the book. This picture was taken at the ex-employees reunion meeting at the Bradford Industrial Museum in August 2012 (Roy Sumpner)

The 1923 Jowett Sports Registered KU 1926. Mike Koch-Osborne

This car is seen at rallies on a regular basis, Mike has prepared some notes which he displays in front of the car, so I feel I can do no better than reproduce his notes here. NS

KU 1926 was built by Jowett to the personal specification of Major J. D. Johnstone of Glen Stuart, Cummertrees, Dunfries.

Major Johnstone had trialled a Jowett, registered AK 9129 for at least two years prior to taking delivery of this car on 26 April 1923, and just eleven days later, on 7 May, he took part in the Scottish Six Day Trial winning a gold medal. Later that month he competed in the London to Edinburgh Run and in 1924 took part in the Land's End to London Trial.

KU 1926 was eventually sold to Bob Grant of Dumfries on 30 November 1926 and was trialled and rallied by him for over fifty years with the exception of nine years when it was on loan to the Sword Collection in Kilmarnock between 1955 and 1964.

For the car to remain competitive it was upgraded over the years and 1929 style wheels and wings were fitted in the 1930s. Although many of these are not standard for a 1923 Jowett, they were original equipment to this particular competition car.

On Bob's death at the age of ninety-six in 1991, it was passed to his son, Harris, who died in 1998.

It was then purchased in June 2002 after seventy-five years of continuous ownership in the same family, ironically by William Jowett's grandson, its present owner.

The next two pictures feature a 1927 Long-Two tourer which I spotted on a Jowett Car Club trip to the Isle of Man in September 2011. This car has been fully restored and looks good even though it was a very wet and windy weekend the whole time we were there!

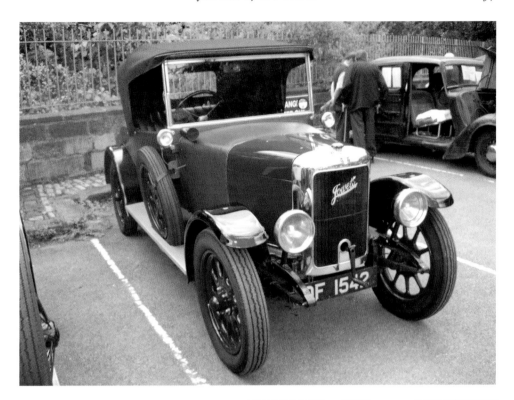

Two pictures of a beautifully restored fabric-bodied 1927 Long-Two tourer, pictured at the Jowett Car Club Ex-Employees Meeting at the Bradford Industrial Museum in August 2008.

A well-known example of a 1927 Long-Two tourer, this is one of the exhibits in the Bradford Industrial Museum, they have a large collection of Jowetts on display, this being one of them. The museum also has a fantastic display of woolen mill machinery and a period mock-up of a Jowett garage and is well-worth a visit.

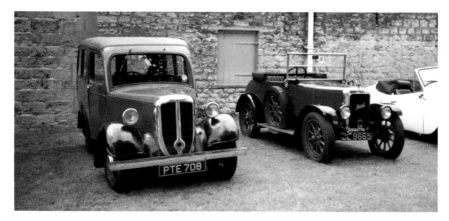

There is a gap of twenty-six years between this 1927 Short-Two and my 1953 Bradford Utility yet mechanically there is very little difference between them. The Bradford was the stop-gap model which was introduced just after the war in 1946 and was pre-war in design in every aspect. The idea was to bring money into the company coffers to help pay for the development costs of the all-new Javelin saloon which was launched in 1947, taking the motoring world by storm. In 1950, the Jupiter sportscar was also produced and was also greeted with great acclaim. It went on to win its class in Le Mans in 1950, 51 and 52 – the only years it was entered. Ironically, it was only the Bradford commercial range that made money for Jowetts after the war and up to closure of the company in 1954. The flat-twin, horizontally-opposed engine in the Bradford was basically the same as the engine in the first Jowett car of 1906, which was used right through the 1920s and 1930s. It was listed in the Guinness Book of Records for many years as being the engine with the longest production run of forty-six years.

This 1927 Short-Two is another beautifully restored car which lives in Devon. This is owned by the chairman of the Jowett Car Club and is a regular attendee to Club rallies.

Two views of another 1927 Short-Two.

These are two views of Ian Priestley's 1927 Full-Four. This car was restored by Ian in 1990 and looks great in maroon and black.

'A SMALL SALOON on YORKSHIRE HILLS: Trying out a fully laden 7hp Jowett with a roomy closed body on some severe gradients in the North Country', *The Autocar*, 18 February 1927

Only a few years ago the motorist of small means was satisfied with an open two-seater car provided that it would take him with reasonable certainty over any class of road or hill that he was likely to meet in his ordinary travels. Indeed, the time is comparatively recent when it seemed that the manufacturers had provided more than was expected, when they sold, for round about £150, a two-seater car of from 7-9hp which would indeed 'go anywhere'. Then came the inevitable moment when someone found that the two-seater would take four people fairly well, and so the public asked that the small-engine 'economy car' should be a successful four-seater. And when the industry nobly responded, and demand for more again arose. 'If a small engine can pull a load of four adults with ease, surely we can have a small saloon', said Mr. Everyman. And so the small saloon has come into being.

A Full Four-Seater

The car which forms the subject of this article is, by virtue of its small cylinder capacity and low price, a 'small saloon', but it must not be overlooked at the outset that the Jowett, as a closed car, is in rather a distinct class. It offers full accommodation four adults. There is more leg room, for instance, in the rear seats than in many 12-15hp closed cars, while the front passenger, if of normal height, has really to stretch in order to reach the dashboard ramp with his feet. Nor is this amount of room consequent upon having high seats as in certain cars of American design. Seats in the Jowett saloon are quite low, so that one is comfortably placed without having the knees bent unduly – in fact; one has very much the arm-chair feeling. This amount of room is obtained by virtue of the fact that the body is fairly long in itself, and the engine, being a horizontally opposed two-cylinder, is exceptionally short. To some degree the arrangement is unusual in that practically all the leg room for the front seats is under the scuttle, consequently the steering wheel is very close to the instrument board, and the driver and front passenger have their faces quite close to the screen. This results in an amazingly wide and unobstructed angle to vision being provided, which is distinctly pleasant.

There are two doors only, both on the near side, and although these are fairly wide, access to the front seats is not particularly easy, although the rear seats are quite good in this respect. It is easily possible for the off-side rear passenger to enter or leave the car while the nearside passenger remains seated, without acrobatics on the part of either.

Well-arranged Controls

The next and an exceedingly favourable impression is that the controls are remarkably well placed; for example, if one steers with the left hand and drops the right hand negligently it will come automatically to the brake lever or gear lever knob, both close together but neither interfering with the other. If the hand is on the gear lever knob while the second gear is engaged, the ignition control on the side of the body can be operated by stretching out a finger, while the oil indicator button can be felt, or the horn button depressed, by a slight upward movement of the hand from the ignition control.

The Jowett has no hand throttle control or carburettor adjustments of any kind brought up the instrument board other than a strangler wire to facilitate starting; thus control is of the simplest.

For our test a full load of four adults weighing approximately forty stones was carried, the car weight being 12cwt, and a route was selected which involved considerably more severe climbing than the average owner of a small saloon would choose to negotiate. The car tested was not a new one and had certain experimental features about the engine which might be expected to result in a higher performance than standard as regards speed, but not necessarily in a better climbing performance. Another car with a quite normal engine also accompanied us, carrying a full load of rather heavier passengers.

Once on the run the car showed extraordinary powers of engine revolutions, for on second gear it attained 42mph on the level (with a fairly good following wind), while the top gear was not much more, being about 46mph. The speedometer was timed to be accurate aver a mile at 30mph. Leathley Bank, a well-known Yorkshire hill near Otley, a stiff climb of over half a mile, culminating at a start pitch of about 1 in 7, resulted in bottom gear on the last section, and a speed of about 15mph on this. A halt was called until the second car arrived, for it had been outpaced on the level, although it climbed well. A steady speed of 35 to 38mph was maintained for most of the run, which is perhaps slightly in excess of average performance; 30 to 35mph being the usual comfortable touring speeds of the Jowett.

An Extreme Test

Good average running over a decidedly 'heavy' route followed to Ripon, and then over the well-surfaced, but twisting road to Thirsk, and on to Sutton Bank. Sutton Bank is a hill that rises for almost a mile; its surface, nowadays, is splendid, but it has a long stretch of a 1 in 4 gradient, and actually averages about 1 in 8 for something like three-quarters of a mile. It is not a hill that the average driver of a small-engined saloon would attempt with a full load, except as a sporting effort. To put the Jowett and its 560lb of human freight at the hill was in the nature of an extreme test, and it should not be taken as a condemnation of the car that it just did not succeed. The low gear ratio, it must be recollected, is only 14.7 to 1, and the task was not altogether fair. The accompanying car also stopped a little higher than the test car, but immediately restarted when its heaviest passenger jumped out. A reshuffle of passengers was made, and with a full compliment of 'lightweights', the test car made a successful climb, although at no great speed over the worst portion of the hill. Meanwhile the original crew watched a 23hp American car make an unsuccessful attempt at the hill.

Both hand and foot brakes were used in the descent, which was perfectly controlled; on a level road it was possible to stop the car from a steady speed of 30mph in a distance of 44 feet – a good performance for a car without front wheel brakes.

Acceleration and Gear Changing

The usual tests of acceleration had to be modified somewhat, as the two-cylinder engine would no pull steadily on top gear at so slow a speed as 10mph. Top gear acceleration, therefore, was tested at a range of 15mph to 30mph, the time being 25 seconds. On second gear the acceleration range from 10mph to 30mph was exceedingly good, several tests being made with results between 13 and 15 seconds.

Gear changing, although quite easy to double clutching, is rather 'heavier' than usual; the absence of a clutch stop necessitates a long wait in changing up, and in consequence, an easy return to a higher ratio is not possible when climbing. The clutch is very good indeed, smooth in take-up and positive; there is only a short traverse on the clutch pedal, the pressure required being fairly heavy.

Brakes, Steering and Comfort

Most ordinary breaking is effected by the rear wheel contracting brakes, the lever of which comes conveniently to hand. This brake is smooth and powerful, and is not affected by wet, as one might imagine an external brake would be. The foot brake contracts on the transmission and is apt to failure if not used gently.

Steering is easy, being decidedly self-centring, and the gearing is of high ratio. Apart from the general roominess of the interior (the height from floor to the roof is 3 feet 11 inches), the car rides nicely, especially if shock absorbers are fitted, and it does not roll unduly when cornering. The interior is snug and free from draughts, while the narrow pillars allow maximum window space and a wide view. It is not noisy except when the engine is running all-out on the indirect gears.

All things considered, the Jowett saloon is a car of remarkable value and wonderful performance for its engine capacity, and it carries four adults in genuine comfort. At a steady 30mph it will bowl along all day, using a gallon of fuel for every 40 miles. Hills with gradients up to 1 in 6 it surmounts with ease, but on exceptional gradients of steeper pitch (there are not many on main roads outside Yorkshire), the gear ratio is slightly too high for a certain ascent with full load.

As we remarked previously, the body is roomy and offers a considerable degree of comfort to the passengers; moreover, the windows, as may be seen in the accompanying illustrations of the car, are particularly large in area and offer commendable interior lighting as well as a maximum visibility for driving purposes – which is a great asset not invariably possessed by closed vehicles, irrespective of class. This comfort and general 'handiness' – even in a car of saloon type, will serve to commend it to the purchaser.

Data for the Driver

7hp two-cylinders horizontally-opposed 75.6mm X 101.5mm, 907cc, Tax £7.
Tested weight of complete car, less passengers, 12cwt. Weight per cc – 1.60 lb.
Gear Ratios, 14.7, 7.4 and 4.56 to 1. Half-elliptic springs front and rear.
Spiral bevel final drive. 27 X 4.40 inch tyres on detachable steel wheels.
Foot-brake on transmission; hand-brake on rear wheels.
Wheelbase 8 feet 6 inches, track 3 feet 9 inches.

Overall height 5 feet 10 inches, length 12 feet, width 4 feet 6 inches.
Fuel consumption, 39-42mpg, tank capacity 6 gallons. Price £185 with saloon body.

William (Bill) Boddy – *Motor Sport* magazine

As mentioned on page 48, Richard Shuttleworth sold one of his Jowetts to Bill Boddy, so I entered into correspondence with Mr Boddy about his Jowetts, he gave details to me about these cars. I was delighted when Mr Boddy reviewed one of my books, *My Car was a Jowett*, in the April 2009 issue of *Motor Sport* as he gave details about them in the review, I am reproducing the part relating to his two cars here, including how he bought the Richard Shuttleworth Long-Two Jowett. N.S.

I have owned two vintage Jowetts and much respected their flat-twin 907cc power units – 'The little engine with the big pull'. My two vintage Jowetts were a 1923 short-two and a 1925 long two-seater. The first I saw advertised for £3 in a breaker's yard with a spare back axle in the boot, so instead of returning to Farnborough, Hampshire, by train, I bought it and it took me back faithfully. Untaxed, none of the police cars I saw seemed to notice me, and I could claim that the licence papers were in the post, as it was Boxing Day (I was escaping from the partying and could post them the next day). The other, the long two-seater, was the ex-Dick Shuttleworth one which Joe Lowrey, also at the RAE, towed back from Bigglesworth on a tow bar behind his HRG.

I tried to start it but it only ran a short distance before stopping. My friends, experts in aero engines, arrived to help. Clean petrol, battery charged, fuel at the carburettor jet – all to no avail. It must have been an ignition fault they said. I then remembered that Delco-Remy had a London depot (until they joined with General Motors) and I asked them if they would check the coil (which had the condenser enclosed within it). They rang back to say that it gave a reasonable spark for such an old coil. I then asked them if they would keep it on test longer. They did and reported that as soon as the thing warmed up it stopped giving a spark. They gave me one of their oil-filled coils which cured the trouble.

I wonder if anyone recalls such a problem, or whether it may help anyone now?

'And if you ask yourself why such utility cars are mentioned in *Motor Sport* you have forgotten the records there by J. J. Hall, a most amusing writer, who with a Jowett two-seater weighing about 8cwt and helped by Horace Grimley, set the class G 12-hour record at 54.89mph in 1928 in spite of having to change three gaskets, the engine having non-standard detachable cylinder heads, giving a 5.25 to 1 compression ratio. The Jowett lapped at 65mph.'

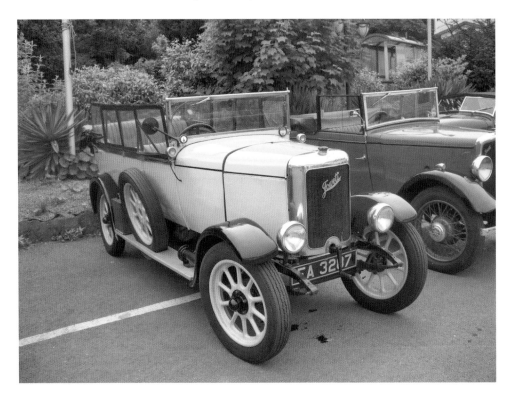

These are two views of a beautifully restored yellow and black 1928 Long-Four.

A Short-Two, this time a 1928 example. This is the only example the author has seen of a Short-Two in white and black.

The Jowett Coupé was one of two new models introduced by Jowett in 1928. This picture is reproduced from the 1928 sales booklet, which describes the car as follows: 'The Jowett Coupé is a dainty edition of a combined Two-Seater and Saloon. Doctors and professional men should examine the snug Coupé.

Exceptionally wide door – no less than 28ins. Wide. Then there is the single panel screen which can be opened by an ingenious screw regulator giving rigidity. A large rear window is provided.

The ingenious dickey is useful both for odd passengers and a host of other things. The Coupé adds fresh laurels to the Jowett name, and maintains the Jowett extraordinary economy in running.'

Only seventy Coupés were built during 1928 and 1929 and, sadly, none is known to have survived.

The Jowett Sports was the other new model introduced by Jowett in 1928; this picture is reproduced from the 1928 sales booklet, which describes the car as follows: 'Youth will be served. The "lads" of nerve and skill looked for an edition of the Jowett two-seater which would *fly*. They will cheer when they see it; slick and trim and "dare devil" as a submarine chaser, with its low-slung body. Leg-roominess has a pull here. The outside hand brake and gear lever handy in a tight corner. All the Jowett ingenuity is here exercised to the last point – a car of speed and beauty.'

Only fourteen Sports models were built in 1928, plus a couple more to special order, but sadly, none of these has survived.

There have been a couple of Sports replicas that have been built which are similar to the original Sports model. But, Ian Priestley, the Club's Pre-War Registrar is building a 1928 Sports Replica at the moment which is a true replica, as it is being built on a 1928 chassis and using correct 1928 mechanical parts. The bodywork has been built using period pictures of the original cars. It is very narrow, only 31 inches wide, and has two offset seats, the passenger one is six inches behind the driver's one. The end result will be excellent and I cannot wait to see it on the road. We just need somebody to recreate a 1928 Coupé now!

The 1928 Jowett Sports Replica registered CB 7818. Ian Priestley

Jowett Cars Ltd introduced the Sports model in 1928 and it was hoped that the car would appeal to the younger man and cost £145 new. Clearly, young men at that time did not think that Jowetts and speedy sports car production went hand in hand as only fourteen of them were built! This was another Jowett model where no survivors were known to exist so Ian and his friend Nigel Stock went out to reconstruct one. This car is a completely correct replica as it uses a 1928 chassis and mechanicals have been used, with Nigel fabricating a body for it.

Ian bought the chassis and dismantled mechanical parts and set about building the replica. As mentioned before, it was a standard 1928 chassis but the radiator, engine and gearbox was set nine inches further back in the chassis which then meant that the propshaft had to be shortened. The steering box was also set back nine inches which meant that the steering column had to be altered. The handbrake and gear lever were fitted outside the bodywork of the car on the original, being mounted on the offside running board. Ian wanted his car to have these controls fitted just the same as the originals which meant some amendments had to be made to the existing controls.

Ian had a few pictures of original Sports models so had to take all measurements from these. The size of the wheels was known so all measurements were worked out from these. Nigel then made a mock-up of the body out of cardboard boxes held together with gaffer tape! They were then able to get the feel of the car and made a few tweaks to the tail, making it longer and sharper. They are now confident that the bodywork will be within one inch of the original, which I think is a fantastic result.

A new hood has also been made for the car, which in turn, has shown a problem the original Sports drivers will have had. The hood has to be down to enable the driver to get into the car, as it has no doors. If the car was parked, and it was raining, the driver would have had to have put the hood down to get in, then erect it again when seated in the car!

Ian attended Beaulieu Autojumble in September 2012 and spotted a pair of headlamps on a bar and thought they would be ideal for the Sports Replica as they fitted perfectly between the wings, so were a great purchase.

The car now needs a bonnet and wings fitted, so it is hoped that the car will be finished later this year. I for one cannot wait to see it!

Top: One of the other Sports models that were produced in 1928 was for Miss Victoria Worsley of Hovingham. She was a very active trials driver during the late 1920s and 1930s. She was very busy during 1928 and 1929 in the Jowett taking part in at least twenty events in 1928 and ten events in 1929, she even raced at Brooklands with it. This car was prepared for her by the Jowett Brothers and was fitted with polished aluminium bodywork. After the Jowett she briefly owned a Bugatti before moving on to racing MGs.

Middle and bottom: A replica of the 1928 Victoria Worsley Sports Special has been built in Australia by John Wilson. It is an exact copy of the original, including the polished aluminium body. John is in the driving seat of one of the pictures. He should be proud of this excellent recreation.

A professional record-breaker called J. J. Hall, who was based in Brooklands, contacted the Jowett brothers in Idle to ask for a special light-weight Jowett sports model to attempt to break the 12-hour Class G record at Brooklands. They were successful in their attempt. Horace Grimley said that the average speed over the twelve hours was 54.64mph, whereas J. J. Hall said it was 54.86mph. In either event, it was just good enough to take the record. This was amazing as the car was lapping at well over 60mph but a lot of time was lost having to replace no less than three cylinder head gaskets during the twelve hours!

Jowett Club member, John Box, built a replica of the 1928 Brooklands record breaker in 1971. I took this picture of the car at Harewood House near Leeds in about 1986. The car was sold to the USA many years ago, so, sadly, I am unlikely to see the car again.

This is the 1928 'Greenhouse' Fabric Saloon bought by Ian Priestley in 1988, the bodywork had been restored but the car needed a full mechanical restoration plus new wings. As can be seen in this picture, the rear wings still needed to be fitted. (Priestley)

The same car as it is today and fully restored, this being the sole survivor out of a production of 266. (Priestley)

THE
"1928"
JOWETT

"For now he's free to sing and play,
over the hills and far away"

R·L Stevenson.

"We are seven"

THE 1928 JOWETT

 what a glory doth this world put on
For him who, with a fervent heart, goes forth
Under the bright and glorious sky ---

Longfellow.

JOWETT CARS LTD.

IDLE, BRADFORD, ENGLAND

'Phone : Idle 341 (3 lines).   *Cables & 'Grams:* "Jowett Cars, Idle"

Page one

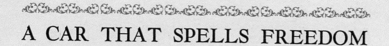

A CAR THAT SPELLS FREEDOM

THE SHORT TWO-SEATER
£134 (*ex works*)

Famous wherever there are hills to climb. Its devotees say that if it had spurs it would climb a tree. Lively in action but delightfully controlled. Business Houses use it for their travellers on account of reliability and small cost of upkeep.

New-type hood and side-curtains; real leather seat and seat-back, hair stuffed over lace-web spring frames; aluminium panelling; dynamo output controlled from dash-board; Standard Dunlop cord balloon tyres and electric starter—a utility car.

Leg-room for the lankiest of drivers. For the shortest too! by reason of adjustable controls.

Page nine

THE 1928 JOWETT

THE LONG TWO-SEATER
£142 *(ex works)*

A real thoroughbred two-seater moulded in every detail to the desire of the motorist. The streaming curve of body opens up into the Dickey Seat where there is ease of limb for outsizes in friends, and yet room for a good tool-locker.

Being a Jowett, there's heaps of room for the six-foot driver, while controls can be adjusted for the petite lady. Door wide—hood weathertight—curtains rigid.

This is a superb two-seater ; in it you can face the wide world with pride (and economy !).

Page ten

THE "NEVER OBSOLETE" CAR

THE CHEERFUL CHUMMY
£142 (*ex works*)

The Chummy is the friendly car. Its accommodation is hardly less than that of most four-seaters.

Although the rear seating is capable of accommodating adults in comfort, it is fine for juveniles, and the springing is arranged accordingly. A swinging portion of the front seat-back gives access to the rear seats. No awkward folding seats.

You can use the hindmost pair of metal-framed side curtains as a rear screen. The ideal car for the lady on a shopping expedition. Chummy! Ready for a friendly lift.

The Commercial Traveller can carry his boxes and cases, snugly protected from the weather.

Page eleven

A 1929 Fabric Long-Saloon; this is often incorrectly described as a 'Black Prince' model. The Black Prince is in fact identical to this car, but of course, it was black! This car is on permanent display at the Bradford Industrial Museum.

This picture was taken in Crieff in May 2008 and shows a 1929 Long-Two on the left with a 1927 Short-Two in the middle and a 1922 Short-Two on the right.

Two shots of a 1929 Long-Two also pictured at the Jowett Car Club National Rally in Crieff, Scotland, in May 2008.

A nice grey and black 1929 Long-Four.

This page and next page above: Another beautifully restored 1929 Long-Four, this time in maroon and black.

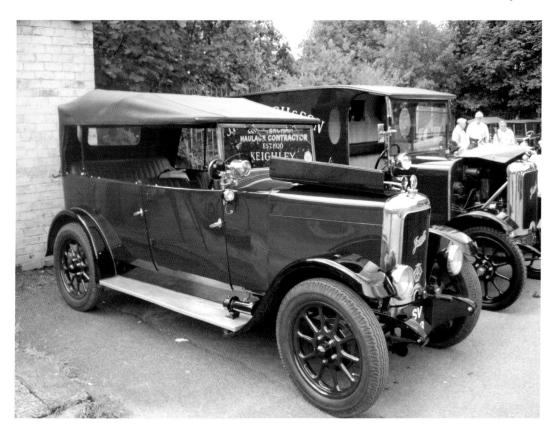

Ian Priestley's 1929 7/17hp Light Four Economy model. This was Jowett's attempt at building a £100 car; in this respect they failed as it was sold new at £110. This is the sole survivor out of the 297 built. (Priestley)

This boat-tailed Jowett started life as a 1929 Long Saloon, so is a sight the Jowett brothers would not have seen themselves. Apparently, when this car was restored recently by Nigel Stock, the bodywork was in a very poor state so the decision was taken to make it into a boat-tailed four-seater tourer. And why not is what I say, similar designs have been built onto Rolls-Royce, Bentley, Talbot and Hispano-Suiza chassis so why not a Jowett! I saw this car for the first time at the Jowett Centenary Rally in Bingley in 2010 and I thought the restoration and the woodwork had been done to the highest standard and the car looked excellent.

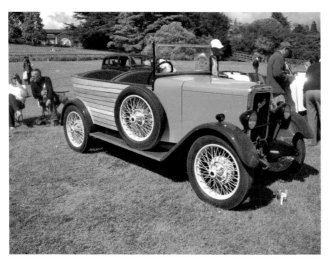

This 1929 Long-Two is Mike Koch-Osborne's latest acquisition and is seen here at the Falcon Manor at the Northern Section of the Jowett Car Club's High Tea get-together on 7 April 2013. This model had the spare wheel on the back of the car, as 1929 saw the added luxury of a driver's door! 1929 was also the first year that Jowett cars were fitted with four wheel brakes, as prior to this brakes were only fitted to the rear wheels.

'4,000 Miles with a Jowett', *The Autocar*, 10 August 1923

Somewhere about ten years ago there began to filter down to the South, strange tales from Bradford of a car of infinitesimally small engine size but of astounding power and longevity. Its name was Jowett.

So unconscionably long were these early Jowetts said to be in dying, or even feeling sick, that legends became current that the Bradford owners were wont to bequeath them, in their wills, as family heirlooms. Whether owing to this sturdy reputation, or whether because of a limited output, it would seem, in delving among the early Jowett records, that few, if any, of these cars were allowed to escape from their native fastnesses. Indeed, it was not until the Six Days Trials, organised by the Edinburgh & District M.C.C. in 1921, that rumour became fact.

The performance of the little 7hp two-cylinder cars in those fierce tests up and down the Highland glens was so outstandingly good that, literally in a week, the Jowett sprang from the possession of a high local reputation to a place in the wider horizon of car fame. Since then these cars have been observed on Southern roads in considerably increased numbers, and their popularity is unquestionable.

It happened that in the first week in January of this year one of these two-seater models came into the possession of the writer. Knowing nothing whatsoever of the car or its performance, and taking delivery in the rather unorthodox manner of going to Nottingham from London and picking up the car there in a garage where the driver from Jowett Cars Ltd, Idle, Bradford, had left it (he had betaken himself back to his native city before he could be interviewed), the owner-driver-writer merely filled it up with fuel, started the engine, and was, in company with a passenger and some luggage, transported via Leicester, Northampton, and St Albans to his home in N.W. London, between the hours of 9.30 a.m. and 3 p.m., passing the while, for the space of one hour, for lunch on the way. A four-seater has since been used for over 1,000 miles, and bids fair to show even better service than the two-seater.

Since then the two-seater has run over 3,000 miles. It can be said of it that it goes just as well as when new, it never needs attention, it has given no trouble. There have been no road stops or punctures. In short, the little car is a road train. The more one drives it the more one appreciates the sound common sense of the small car owners of Bradford in assimilating all they can get from the Jowett factory. Of course, a new and properly made car ought not give trouble during the first few thousand miles. But, alas, quite a number do, in greater or lesser degree. The Jowett has not even needed a spanner to be applied to it anywhere.

So much for reliability. With regard to its speed, the maximum by the Smith speedometer is approximately 45 mph. It undoubtedly shows its best pace when it is somewhat heavily laden; for instance, two adults, a child, and some luggage seem to form the ideal load. It keeps the car down on the road and makes the engine work, which it does very smoothly.

There is, of course, never a rose without a thorn – in fact, quite a number of thorns in some cases – and it must not be pretended that the Jowett is a perfect small car. Probably such an article does not exist in this imperfect world. There are two points which may fairly be criticised. First, the steering, which though light and fairly positive, is not so precise as one could wish. It consists of a pinion meshing with an internally toothed ring, and provision is made to take up wear. It is a special design peculiar to the car, and, while satisfactory as a means of direction the car is a little liable to wander about the road if attention is diverted.

Good Equipment

Next, the front and rear half-elliptic springs are somewhat on the flexible side, but a pair of Gianoli shock absorbers in the front worked wonders and improved the steering. This applies to the two-seater.

Referring to the general equipment, the coachwork is so good as to be worthy of a really expensive machine. All the panelling is aluminium, the upholstery is real leather, the seat wide and deep, and the back is arranged at a very comfortable angle. There is a large dickey seat provided which will seat two people if needed, and the seat of the dickey is removable, giving a great quantity of space for luggage. The instrument board is of polished mahogany, with flush fitting instruments, comprising of the Brolt ammeter and switches for the ignition and lighting, and the belt-driven Smith's speedometer.

With regard to the whole question of engines for a very small car there will probably, for many years to come, be a discussion as to whether the miniature four or the flat-twin will prevail. Each type has its good points and its drawbacks. The flat-twin water-cooled engine of 75.4mm bore and 101.5mm stroke (907cc) of the Jowett is an extremely good example of this class. There is every reason why it should be, as the makers have been continuously developing this particular type for the last twelve years or so. It is, to all intents and purposes, vibration-less, and a pencil can be balanced upright on the radiator cap with the engine running light.

The Four Seater

At speeds from about 20 to 33mph there is no perceptible vibration whatever, and as regards smoothness of running at normal speeds it would be difficult to say whether the power unit had two or four cylinders. The engine possesses in a marked degree the excellent attribute of all flat-twins – the power to hang on to top gear on hills. Its performance on quite severe gradients on top gear (4.5 to 1) is one of the outstanding features of the car. Its second speed of 7.4 to 1 gives a distinctly useful performance on gradients up to about 1 in 9 and on low gear of 14.7 to 1 one imagines that it would take something in the nature of a precipice to stall the car.

Extreme care is evidently taken to ensure very free movement of all parts, and the Jowett compares remarkably well with other cars, both large and small, of the writer's acquaintance in its coasting abilities. Indeed it is astonishing the distances the car will travel on a level road when suddenly slipped into neutral at a road speed of about 20mph. This is a very good test to impose upon any car, as it proves not only that no brakes are binding, but also that the bearings in the transmission and wheels are running perfectly free.

Well Arranged Cooling System

The engine is too efficiently cooled to give the best results, though possibly this super-cooling might be exceedingly useful to owners living in a really hilly district. The thermo-syphon cooling is arranged on the theoretically ideal principle of perfectly horizontal return pipes from the base of the radiator to the cylinders, and straight outlet pipes allowing a remarkably good head of water from the cylinders to the radiator. This is one of the points in which the flat-twin engine scores over the four-cylinder, in that it automatically provides the designer with a simple and efficient layout for the water system. The interesting discussion which took place some little time ago in *The Autocar* regarding pump and thermo-syphon cooling for small engines could not very well apply to the Jowett, because where the water circulated by pump and the present radiator used, there is no doubt that the engine would never attain anything like a satisfactory working temperature.

The oil consumption works out at about 750 to 800 miles per gallon. The writer has found that a very light-bodied oil appears to suit the force-feed system of the Jowett remarkably well. The same oil is used for the gears and for the back axle; it is quite unnecessary to use anything heavier for either of these components. Half a pint in the gearbox every 500 miles is advisable.

Good Weather Protection

The little car is equipped with a leather cloth hood and side shields which open and close with the doors, and in the heaviest rain it is absolutely weatherproof.

The makers are wise in providing a large look-out celluloid window in the back of the hood, a point much appreciated when driving in traffic with the hood up.

Up to last year ignition on the Jowett was by magneto, but this year the makers have adopted Delco-Remy battery and coil with Brolt lamps and switchboard. With this system starting is ridiculously easy.

With regards to the brakes, that operated by pedal consists of a Ferodo-lined contracting band, operating on a drum behind the gear box, while the right-hand side hand-operated brake causes Ferodo-lined bands to contract on generous-sized drums mounted on the rear axle. Both brakes are extremely powerful, and, indeed, it is well to use the foot brake with a certain amount of caution, as it is easy to lock the wheels and skid the tyres by its use. Powdered graphite renders it smoother.

Since the above experiences were written, the writer has covered a thousand miles on a four-seater Jowett. This model is precisely similar to the two-seater, except that the wheelbase was 18 inches longer, namely 8 feet 6 inches, and a Brolt electric starter is fitted.

Gear ratios are the same as on the two-seater, and with four adults on board there is remarkably little difference in the road performance. With three or four up, the springing is very good and is probably kept at its best by a set of Jeavons spring gaiters which have been fitted. A considerably larger battery is supplied to cope with the electric starting, and the higher-bonneted car is more imposing in appearance than the two-seater.

Cheap Family Motoring

The performance on the road is a striking testimony to what a miniature engine of sound design and construction can do in the way of serious work. The body is very well made, has two doors and lots of leg- room; indeed a driver of abnormal height is perfectly comfortable in the front seats. The all-weather curtains are very efficient when erected, and when out of use are carried in a compartment behind the rear seats. Grease gun lubrication is supplied.

The only point of criticism which can be fairly advanced is that the tyres fitted as standard are not big enough for best appearance or maximum comfort, though, up to the present, they show no signs of wear. They are 650 X 65mm Dunlop cords. If 700 X 80mm, or better still, 710 X 90mm tyres were fitted, the car would be almost uncriticisable as a light, roomy, inexpensive vehicle, capable of carrying quite large loads at a reasonable speed over long distances at a ridiculously low cost.

THE NEW
LONG TWO-SEATER
JOWETT

If ever a car could be described as " made to fill a long-felt want," this is that car. Longsight, not lack of foresight, prevented us from offering it in the past, for had we not to complete our range of economy cars, before turning our efforts towards a more luxurious car ? Came the two-seater in 1910, redesigned in 1921, next the four-seater two years later, and the light four in 1924. Ungracious winters then necessitated a Saloon which we produced in 1925—and then you "had us," for at last we had entered the luxury market—or so you said, and still more vehemently demanded a long two-seater. Well, ladies and gentlemen,—here it is !

JOWETT CARS, IDLE, BRADFORD

Of course you will want to know how many of your ideas we have embodied in this car. Well, there is the long, low bonnet and scuttle dash that seems just made to be headed towards " the land of where you will " : there is a high double screen running the full width of the car, with a rubber-sealed rain gutter, where upper meets lower glass : then a wide door to give you easy access to the more than roomy seats, which are deeply upholstered in blue leather, and wide enough for two " outsize " people, wide enough to allow change of position on a long ride.

Leg-room on a Jowett goes without saying. There's more than enough for 6-ft. passengers, yet little enough for Miss five-foot-two, thanks to adjustable controls.

A hood that fits like a glove round the screen and metal-framed side curtains, but high and wide and deep so that there is ample air to avoid any possibility of stuffiness. And it gives ample clearance behind the passengers to avoid that irritation of constantly touching the back of the hat.

Rear of the seats and before the hood, the body forms a useful shelf for holding small parcels and the loose impedimenta of the tour.

J O W E T T   C A R S ,   I D L E ,   B R A D F O R D

It's a gracious car this long two-seater, for was it not moulded to your own desires?

But what have we done with all the space you know must be left, even after providing passenger comfort only associated with Jowetts and the larger luxury cars? We have provided a boot capable of holding no less than five suit cases. Your golf bag (and your friend's) can be housed with the lid closed. Then there is a removable dickey seat, good and wide— not a shelf on which to perch your friend, but a seat he can occupy in comfort the day long, if needs be, or you so desire. The upholstered lid forms a comfortable backrest at just the right angle, and his knees are inside the body, not bumping his chin. Six foot leg-room, again, of course.

But we are not finished yet. The gracefully curved rear end of the body forms a fine big tool locker, capable of holding far more kit than is ever required for a Jowett on the longest tour. Thus we have used all our space just as you would have us do. But did we not start out to build this car for you? And are not these your own ideas? Truly then, it is a car of creature comforts, at a price you never dreamed possible.

JOWETT CARS, IDLE, BRADFORD

'Driving the 7hp Jowett to the Best Advantage: Hints on starting up, changing gear and generally controlling the more popular makes of light car', *The Light Car & Cyclecar*, 6 July 1928

The Jowett is unique in that it is the only car of its type on the British market today having a two-cylinder engine. Motorists who have never driven one of these cars sometimes ask if the two-cylinder engine makes it more difficult to handle than a four-cylinder job. Admittedly, a 'two-lunger' calls for slightly different driving methods, but the car is certainly just as easy to manage.

Let us begin at the beginning, however, and consider starting. The great thing to remember is that it is not advisable to 'swing' the engine – that is, give the handle several continuous turns. What should be done is to engage the handle as near as possible at the top of the down stroke and give it a sharp push down and pull up. If it does not fire, another and entirely separate attempt on the same lines should be made.

So much for the several manipulation of the handle. There is now the setting of the controls to be considered. The Jowett is fitted with coil ignition; for starting, the switch may be set either in the 'half' or 'full-charge' position – it does not matter which – and the advance and retard control should be set to full retard. If the engine is cold the strangler will have to be fully closed, and the carburettor may be flooded – not excessively – with advantage.

It is advisable to turn the engine over slowly twice to suck in a rich mixture, and on the third to turn briskly, when the engine should fire, and the driver can walk round to the driving seat and gradually open the strangler control a little at a time until the normal supply of air can be safely given.

No hand throttle is fitted, and in very cold weather the engine will sometimes start, only to peter out almost immediately. When the electric starter is used this, of course, can be avoided, as the driver will be sitting at the controls and can depress the accelerator slightly; but when the engine is being started by hand this cannot be done.

A simple way out of the difficulty is to lift the side of the bonnet, pull the control rod to open the throttle slightly and slip a piece of paper about as thick as a tram ticket between the adjusting screw on the throttle arm and the stop on the body of the carburettor. This, of course, will have the effect of opening the throttle slightly, and there will be no need to lift the bonnet again to remove the paper, because it will automatically drop out when the throttle is opened.

So soon as the engine is running, a glance should be given at the oil-pressure gauge; this takes the form of a small plunger – just to the right of the steering column – and it is pushed out so soon as any pressure is built up in the lubrication system. When the engine is running the plunger should always be fully out, and if it is not in the position investigations must be made immediately to find out the reason.

Gear changing is very simple, although double declutching is, of course, advisable when changing down. The best speeds for changing up in the ordinary way are graphically shown on the opposite page. Naturally, for a very quick getaway, the engine should be revved up slightly more on bottom and second gears before changing.

The Jowett engine has a fairly high compression ratio, and this, coupled with the fact that it is of the two-cylinder type, makes it very sensitive to the ignition control. This is quite accessibly placed, and it pays to make full use of it, advancing gradually as the engine accelerates and, conversely, retarding slowly as the speed of the car drops in top gear on the steep hill. So as soon as a change down is made and the engine speed increases once more, the control should be set to full advance again.

The excellent feature of the car is the dynamo output control, and by judicious use of this an owner can always keep the battery well up to the mark and, at the same, prolong its life by avoiding overcharging. During the summer, when little use is made of the lamps, it was found that 'half charge' will keep the battery well 'up', unless of course, the car is used for very short runs, with frequent calls upon the electric starter. In the winter 'full charge' will probably be needed almost all the time if the car is used for town work.

Finally, a word about the brakes; both foot and hand take effect on the rear wheels, the former through the medium of a drum on the transmission and the latter by means of contracting bands on the wheel drums. If the transmission brake becomes fierce, undue strains will be set up in the final drive and the fabric universal joint and the bevels may eventually suffer; the fault should therefore be corrected immediately by applying four or five drops of oil on the drum.

On a very long hill it is advisable to use the hand and foot brakes in turn to avoid throwing all the work on the transmission brake and possibly causing the band to overheat. Alternatively, the hand brake may be kept partly 'on' by means of the ratchet, the pedal being used to obtain the extra braking effect needed.

'Road Test showing principal characteristics of the 7-17hp Jowett Short Saloon', *The Motor*, 26 February 1929

One of the first light cars ever to be produced, the 7-17hp Jowett has built up an indeed enviable reputation for reliability and consistency in running, extending over a period of many years. It is available now in two forms, namely, a long chassis and a short chassis, there being a range of models listed at under £150; these include a short four-seater at £110 5s, a short saloon at £130; long two-seater at £142, and long four-seater at £141 in fabric finish (the coachbuilt-finished model costing £144).

The model tested was the short saloon, the bodywork of which was exceptionally good, especially when one takes into consideration the low initial cost. The front seats are separate and will accommodate comfortably persons of average height, whilst, thanks to the well provided in the back, adult passengers can be carried without undue camping. The car is naturally ideal for the family man, as the back compartment is particularly suitable for children. Two wide doors and tip-up front seats provide easy access to the rear seats.

The driving position is very good, the steering wheel being well raked and placed quite close to the driver, whilst the controls fall readily to hand; a central gear lever is provided, the hand brake being located on the right. The steering is direct, but not unduly heavy, and one very soon becomes accustomed to the small movements needed to manoeuvre the car.

The Jowett is unique insomuch as it is the only car on the British market with a horizontally opposed twin-cylinder engine, which is really surprisingly smooth. In fact, contrary to what one might first expect from an enclosed car with this type of engine, the short saloon is quite pleasant to travel in, and after a long journey the occupants had no greater feeling of tiredness or strain than is experienced in many a much more expensive car. The power unit veritably lives up to the maker's slogan, 'The little engine with the big pull.' Naturally, the acceleration from 10mph is not quite so smooth as with a four-cylinder power unit, but from 15mph or so the getaway is good.

The maximum speed on the model tested was just over 40mph, but it had not been fully run-in, after which period, however, the car should be capable of over 45mph.

On second gear the performance is good also, 10 to 20mph being covered in 6 seconds, and 30mph from 10mph in 12 seconds, whilst on this ratio it has a maximum speed of 32mph. Even with the engine revving hard at this speed there was no feeling of roughness; the gearbox also was notably quiet. The gear change, incidentally, is easy.

The cruising speed is between 35mph and 40mph, at which speeds it will maintain happily for mile after mile without any apparent effort or producing undue fatigue upon the driver.

As a hill-climber the Jowett excels, and, whilst it will take the average main-road gradient quite comfortably without resorting to a lower ratio, it will readily ascend any steep acclivity without the slightest effort if in due use be made of the gearbox. Even long climbs on the intermediate ratio produced no signs of stress or boiling. The short chassis has rear-wheel and transmission brakes only, and these take effect rather harshly, but by judicious application they will bring the car to a standstill without locking the wheels in reasonably good distances.

The saloon tested was supplied by F.O.C.H. Ltd, Heath Street, Hampstead, London, NW, who are the London distributors.

Car Tested – 7-17hp Jowett Short Saloon, price £130, tax £7.
Speed in Gears – Top (4.55 to 1) 45 – 50mph; 2nd (7.45 to 1), 32 – 33mph; 1st (14.75 to 1), 16mph; minimum speed in top 10mph. Petrol Consumption – 45-50mph.
Turning Circle – Right, 33 feet, left 35 feet. Weight – As tested with two up 13¼ cwt.

'Amazing Jowett Performance', *The Light Car & Cyclecar*, 29 November 1929

Can a 7hp car tow a trailer weighing 32 tons? A fortnight ago the answer might have been a decided negative, and when the question is propounded again in the terms of the Jowett saloon and the Dyson 32-wheeled 110 ton trailer – which weighs 32 tons, and of which the ball bearings alone weigh considerably more than the Jowett

– it might be described as fantastic. Godfrey's Ltd, of 366 Euston Road, NW1 – the sole London agents for Jowetts – thought otherwise; however, and looking from the Jowett stand to the neighbouring Dyson stand at the Commercial Motor Show, they expressed the conviction that alone and unaided the Jowett was capable of moving the gigantic trailer from rest, and towing it along!

The attempt was duly made on 20 November in the yard of the Pickford's Garage, Tower Bridge Road, the yard having a level concrete surface. The trailer was suitably coupled up by wire hawsers to the rear of the secondhand 1929 Jowett saloon which was to perform the 'impossible', and on the word 'go', without any extra weight in the saloon, or anything approaching outside aid, the enormous trailer jerked forward, and was towed across the yard, as far as space would permit!

After this astonishing feat, the Jowett was scrupulously examined, and it was found that it has sustained no obvious strain or damage of any kind. This must surely rank as one of the most extraordinary tests ever successfully carried out.

Acknowledgements

The Francis Frith Collection
LAT Photographic
Richard Jones of www.oldclassiccar.co.uk – This is a great website and well-worth a look!
Surrey Vintage Vehicle Society – Check out their excellent website as well – www.svvs.org
The Shuttleworth Collection
Richard Shuttleworth – An Illustrated Biography by Kevin Desmond
The Complete Jowett History by Paul Clarke & Ed Nankivell
The Jowett Car Club Archive
The Autocar magazine
The Motor magazine
The Light Car & Cyclecar magazine

As with all my previous books, I would like to thank my wife, Jane, for her continued support and understanding for all things Jowett. Also to my children, Jonathan, Jessica and Ben, all of whom have children of their own now, who are all Junior members of The Jowett Car Club! Also to my son-in-law, Liam, who helps me with my computer problems and picture copying.

I would also like to thank the contributors to the 'Some Jowett Owners of Today' section of the book giving details of their vehicle restorations, Richard Gane, Michael Koch-Osborne, Vic Morrison, Mike Eames and John Box. Last, but not least, to my good friend and mentor in all things Jowett, Ian Priestley, who has been involved with so many restorations over the years.

Other titles by Noel Stokoe:

Jowett 1901–1954 (Images of Motoring), ISBN: 0752417231
My Car was a Jowett, ISBN: 0752427960
Jowett – Advertising the Marque, ISBN: 0752435353
Sporting Jowetts, ISBN: 9780752447759
Jowett – A Century of Memories, ISBN: 9781445600871